AFRICAN AMERICANS AND JEWISH AMERICANS

AFRICAN AMERICANS
AND
JEWISH AMERICANS

A History of Struggle

by Hedda Garza

THE AFRICAN-AMERICAN EXPERIENCE

FRANKLIN WATTS
A Division of Grolier Publishing
New York / London / Hong Kong / Sydney
Danbury, Connecticut

For Yolanda Axelrod,
my Jewish second mother,
a brave survivor of Auschwitz.

And for "Pie" Prunty,
my African American sister,
who raised her seven children alone and taught me to keep
on going and smiling—no matter what.

May we all live to see a world
of genuine freedom and equality!

Frontis: Jewish American Mickey Schwerner (standing) and two African American volunteers to the "Freedom Summer" campaign, in which many Jewish Americans and African Americans worked together.

Photographs copyright ©: Richard Woodley: pp. 2, 151; The Bettman Archive: pp. 19, 71, 109, 125; National Park Service, Augustus Sherman Collection: p. 45; UPI/Bettmann: pp. 61, 63, 75, 88, 89, 132, 143, 147, 152, 154.

Library of Congress Cataloging-in-Publication Data

Garza, Hedda.
    African Americans and Jewish Americans: a history of struggle / by Hedda Garza.
        p. cm. — (The African-American experience)
    Includes bibliographical references and index.
    ISBN 0-531-11217-9 (lib. bdg.)—ISBN 0-531-15798-9 (pbk.)
    1. Afro-Americans—Relations with Jews—Juvenile literature. 2. Afro-Americans—History—Juvenile literature. 3. Jews—United States—History—Juvenile literature. 4. United States—Race relations—Juvenile literature. 5. United States—Ethnic relations—Juvenile literature. I. Title. II. Series.
E185.G23   1995
973'.04924—dc20   95-18838
                                                                      CIP   AC

CONTENTS

ACKNOWLEDGMENTS

A very special thanks to Constance Pohl, my patient and talented editor at Franklin Watts, who through her knowledge of history and her perseverance always makes my books better. And to Jim Cockcroft, whose perceptive comments and careful reading contribute so much to my work—and whose love helps me to climb over every stumbling block.

INTRODUCTION

More than thirty years after Martin Luther King, Jr., intoned his famous "I have a dream" speech, more than three-quarters of African Americans reportedly believe that society is unfair to blacks. Almost half have lost hope for equality in the future, and almost a quarter say it will never come.[1]

The nation's economic stagnation since 1973 caused some people to expect a rebirth of protest movements. African Americans and their white allies would march in the streets again, they thought, demanding that the government invest in a large-scale plan to rebuild the sagging economy. Millions of people would be put to work revamping schools, wiping out the slums, inaugurating a far-reaching health plan, cleaning up the environment. The idea made economic sense, too: fix the leaking roof to prevent the collapse of the house. The money would be spent now so that billions of dollars in the future could be saved that would otherwise go down the drain of expanded police forces and still more prisons and drug rehabilitation centers. Even more important, an end would come to the horrible waste of human lives.

Instead, the opposite happened. "Blame the victim" became the number one hit song of the day, as "You can make it if you really try" became a national media theme. The old story of Little Toot, "the little engine that could," was put forth in dozens of new "inspirational" versions. On television screens, blind people painted, one-legged people ran in marathons, and poverty-stricken high school dropouts went on to become brain surgeons. The implication was clear: impoverished

African Americans and others were suffering because they hadn't tried hard enough.

Worse yet, an old and ugly twin disease gained ground— blatant racism and overt acts of anti-Semitism. During the presidential election campaign of 1988, most political analysts agreed that George Bush's racist "Willie Horton" television advertisement, showing a black convict released on a prison furlough and quickly committing another violent crime, had much to do with Bush's victory. The publication of Bob Haldeman's diaries shortly after former president Richard M. Nixon's death in 1994 simply repeated what was already known during the time of the Watergate scandal: the Nixon White House had seethed with antiblack and anti-Jewish hatred. Nixon had told Haldeman that he was "Pretty fed up with blacks and their hopeless attitude" and that his idol Billy Graham had told him "there are Satanic Jews and that's where our problem arises."[2]

Far more surprising was a flood of anti-Semitic rhetoric from some self-proclaimed black leaders. First, there was a scandal at City College of New York when the head of the black studies department, Professor Leonard Jeffries, was accused of teaching anti-Semitism to his students. A Jewish City College professor, Michael Levin, dusted off old allegations of a scientific basis for a supposed genetic inferiority of blacks. This kind of inflamed bigotry was reinforced in the mid-1990s by a torrent of abuse against Jews and Catholics from spokesmen of the Nation of Islam, a Black Muslim organization. Khalid Abdul Muhammad, senior aide to the organization's leader Louis Farrakhan, made a virulent anti-Semitic speech at Kean College in Union, New Jersey. In a nation often called a "melting pot" and a "gorgeous mosaic," where ethnic foods from tacos to pizza and dim sum are enjoyed by everyone, Muhammad called Jews "hook-nosed, bagel-eating, lox-eating, impostors" and "bloodsuckers." Then he labeled New York City "Jew York City" and said the Holocaust was justified.

Louis Farrakhan's response was "I didn't say it, Khalid did— did he lie?"[3]

Representative Charles B. Rangel, an African American congressman from Harlem, said of Khalid Abdul Muhammad, "We're dealing with a person who is very dangerous, bitter and, in my opinion, very sick." Another member of the congressional Black Caucus, Major Owens of Brooklyn, called the Nation of Islam "a hatemongering fringe group." But that did not explain the large enthusiastic turnouts of black college students to hear Muhammad speak, or the anti-Jewish chants at a February 1994 rally held in rented space at Howard University, the nation's most prestigious black campus.[4]

Despite a not inconsiderable outcry from many black leaders, demands for further black condemnation of Farrakhan's group escalated. In an article entitled "Enforcing Correctness," Christopher John Farley commented, "What rankles some blacks is that some whites feel the need to make *all* black leaders speak out whenever one black says something stupid. Last month Senator Ernest Hollings joked about Africans being cannibals, but no other white senators were pressured to condemn him. Rush Limbaugh and Howard Stern make questionable racial remarks, and yet former president George Bush invited Limbaugh to the White House."[5]

American students at many colleges were enrolled in black studies programs established in the late sixties. Hispanics in Latino studies programs concentrated on Latino history, and Jewish members of Hillel studied Jewish history. Each group studied its own history but rarely knew much about other minority groups. Some educators were pushing for a change in that policy. They were encouraging multicultural curricula from grade school through college so that misconceptions about "the other" could be eradicated. The need for such studies was all the more apparent by 1995.[6]

Blaming minority groups for economic problems is an old game. Powerful policy makers undoubtedly find it an excellent distraction to take the focus off *their* failures.

There is an old and bitter joke told about World War II. It goes like this:

On the streets of Warsaw, Poland, a Nazi soldier, brandishing his weapon, confronts a Jewish man. "Jew! Who started the war?" he bellows.

The man hesitates as though he is mulling over the

question seriously. "The Jews ... and the bicycle riders,"
he slowly says.
   "Why the bicycle riders?" the Nazi demands.
The Jewish man shrugs. "Why the Jews?" he responds.

This story probably never occurred in the real world of Nazi-
occupied Poland. If the Jew had responded sarcastically as he
does in the story, he undoubtedly would have been pistol-
whipped or shot dead on the spot, but the message of the anec-
dote reflects the way all persecuted people feel: Why us?

Paul Parks, an African American soldier from Indianapolis,
understood that clearly when, on April 25, 1945, his segregated
service unit stationed in Germany was sent to a place called
Dachau. As Parks and his platoon moved into a large area surrounded by an electrified barbed-wire fence, skeletal figures
emerged from barracks and embraced the black soldiers.
Nearby was a huge ovenlike building, still hot and filled with
smoldering human bones. All around it were piles of emaciated bodies, left stacked up for burning as the Nazis fled.

While another unit arrived and distributed food and medicine, Parks sat for hours with a rabbi, one of the handful of
emaciated survivors. Horrified and sick at heart, Parks tried to
fathom what he had seen. The story of Europe's concentration
camps had not been part of his basic training. "Why Jews?"
Parks asked the man. "What did they do? Did they fight the
Germans? What did they do?" The rabbi answered, "Nothing."
"It doesn't make sense," Parks responded. "Why were they
killed?" "They were killed because they were Jews," said the
rabbi. Parks sat by the road and thought. "I understand that,"
the twenty-year-old soldier said finally. "I understand that,
because I've seen people lynched just because they were
black."[7]

During that same period, Ernest Borinski, refugee German
Jewish sociologist speaking to his African American students at
Tougaloo College in Mississippi, tried to explain the illogical
phenomenon that had cost so many lives in Europe and in the
United States. He cited the "two great crimes of Jews and
blacks: Jews are not Christians and blacks are not white."[8]

If Professor Borinski were alive today, it is likely that he would endorse Dr. Martin Luther King, Jr.'s views on anti-Semitism and racism. Dr. King, in his famous letter from a Birmingham jail, told his fellow clergymen: "It was 'illegal' to aid and comfort a Jew in Hitler's Germany. Even so, I am sure that, had I lived in Germany at the time, I would have aided and comforted my Jewish brothers."[9]

There can be little doubt that Dr. King would have been horrified by the anti-Semitism among some groups in the black community today. He would have been especially shocked to learn that young black college men and women were buying into the anti-Jewish hatred. He viewed anti-Semitism as "singularly despicable" because "black people, who have torturously burned in the crucible of hatred for centuries, should have become so purified of hate in these scorching flames as to be instinctively intolerant of intolerance."[10]

Dr. King was undoubtedly aware that at least half of the young people who came to the Deep South as volunteers during the Freedom Summer of 1964 were from Jewish families. The Senate had just passed the 1964 Civil Rights Act, and the summer project volunteers were participating in the voter registration drive for blacks who had long been denied this elemental right. As white volunteer workers poured into Mississippi, they grew accustomed to angry Ku Klux Klansmen and other southerners calling all whites who allied with African Americans "Jew Boys" and "Commies." Southern racists believed that the civil rights movement had been created not by blacks yearning for freedom but by Jewish Communist agitators from the North, stirring up "their" black folks.

No one was terribly surprised when the bodies of three murdered civil rights workers were found buried in the Mississippi Delta on August 4, 1964 (see Chapter 7). The three young men—James Chaney, Michael Schwerner, and Andrew Goodman—had disappeared on June 20 while en route to Longdale, Mississippi, to investigate the burning of a black church. Dozens of black civil rights workers had been brutalized, shot, lynched, and "disappeared" for decades—but this time two young whites were also involved. Schwerner and Goodman were not only white; they were Jewish.

A very special kind of tie brought African Americans and

Jewish Americans into alliances to fight a common enemy—prejudice—not only during the civil rights movement, but long before. For generations they had banded together to combat "that combination of inferior status and derogatory thought we call racism."[11] Before the Civil War, the slaves took the biblical stories of the Jews' escape from slavery to freedom as a metaphor for their own eventual release from bondage. The content of the spirituals sung by the slaves is based on the Jewish experience of slavery recorded in the Old Testament.

The story of that long history of friendship between African Americans and Jewish Americans should be part of required multicultural classes in all schools. It is hoped that by telling it here honestly, this book will contribute toward ending the poison of prejudice.

WANTED: KIDNAPPED AFRICANS—NOT WANTED: EXPELLED JEWS

At the time of the American Revolution in 1776, half a million unwilling African "immigrants," most of them slaves, lived in Colonial America. A group of about 2,500 free Jews lived there too. You could say that Christopher Columbus was indirectly responsible for both groups' presence. His "voyage of discovery" in 1492 had led to the introduction of slavery in the colonies and had coincided with the expulsion of the ancestors of the Colonial Jews from Spain.

When Columbus landed on Hispaniola, today's Dominican Republic and Haiti, he quickly spotted gold and Indians. He expected the Indians to provide enough labor to dig out the gold. Instead, most died of brutal work conditions, wholesale slaughter, suicide, and smallpox—all "gifts" brought by their "visitors."[1]

Faced with a shortage of labor, the Spaniards and other Europeans moved quickly into the African slave trading business. Over the next four centuries, anywhere from 20 to 50 million people were stolen from their homes in Africa, chained in the holds of slave ships, and sold as human machines for greedy men.

Advance parties of Spanish explorers brought about a hundred African slaves with them to today's South Carolina in 1526. Almost a century later a larger party of about five hundred English explorers established the Jamestown settlement in Virginia but only sixty survived the first winter. In 1619 twenty slaves were brought to Jamestown and put to work growing corn for subsistence and tobacco for export. The colony expanded as did other colonies along the East Coast. The free labor of slaves proved a highly profitable business proposition. By 1637, only sixteen years after the *Mayflower* arrived at Plymouth, the first Colonial American slave ship, the *Desire*, sailed from Marblehead, Massachusetts. Its hold was outfitted with narrow racks and chest and leg chains.

The supply of African people seemed inexhaustible—an estimated 50 to 100 million spread over several different tribal kingdoms that in many respects were more advanced than the feudal fiefdoms of Europe.[2] Muslim, Arab, and European Christian slave hunters kidnapped as many Africans as they could grab at gunpoint. They also struck deals with some corrupt tribal chiefs to "capture" prisoners previously taken in battles with other tribes. The profits were enormous. One ship captain wrote that the temptation to make money was so great that the slavers became "indifferent to the sufferings of their fellow creatures. It gradually brings a numbness upon the heart."[3]

Olaudah Equiano, the son of the leader of a prosperous agricultural village, was kidnapped from his village in the African kingdom of Benin in 1745 at the age of eleven and taken to the American colonies. Many years later he told about his capture in his autobiography, *The Interesting Narrative of the Life of Olaudah Equiano*, published in 1789. He was one of only a very few slaves who told their stories.

Olaudah was seized by armed men, bound and gagged, and taken to a coastal fort. He was herded into a pen with dozens of other Africans, branded with hot irons with the mark of the slaveship company, marched along with other chained captives to a beach, and thrown into the hold of a ship.

Olaudah fainted at the sight of hundreds of chained black people and of the ship's boiler, blazing like a huge oven. Later he asked someone who spoke his language if he was about to be "eaten by these white men with horrible looks, red faces, and long hair." Things weren't quite that bad, he was told. They were on their way "to these white people's country to work for them."

For weeks the only sounds were the screams and moans of

the ill and dying. Olaudah found it almost impossible to breathe with no windows and the air filled with the stink of human waste. Chained at the wrists and ankles in a narrow bin for weeks, he refused food and was whipped by his overseers. After just a few days of this voyage of hell, the young boy "wished for the last friend, death, to relieve me."[4]

When the ship landed, white planters and merchants came on board to look over the cargo. Olaudah was sold several times over the next few years. His last master, a Philadelphia merchant, allowed him to work for wages and purchase his freedom. Olaudah Equiano was long dead before slavery was abolished.

In 1654, when the first Jews arrived in the American colonies, the phrase "wandering Jew" was already in common use.[5] Long before the birth of Christianity, the Jews, who believed in one God instead of the dozens of gods worshiped in ancient times, had been allowed to live in other people's kingdoms according to the whim of those in charge.

When the Romans burned down the Second Temple in Jerusalem in A.D. 70, the Jews fled to Roman colonies throughout the world. In most places during the Middle Ages, Jews were shoved into overcrowded areas called ghettos, very much like today's worst slums. They were hemmed in by dozens of restrictive laws that made it almost impossible for them to earn a living. They stayed in some countries for decades, but in others, when times were hard, religious fervor was often used as an excuse to blame the Jews for everything and kill them or expel them again. As Christianity spread, the number of safe places for Jews shrank. Labeled "Christ killers" in a superstitious world, Jews became the target of wild rumors that they sacrificed Christian children. In the fourteenth century, even the bubonic plague was blamed on them when the claim spread that they had poisoned the wells.

The ancestors of America's first Jews lived from the eighth to the fourteenth century in Spain and Portugal where, comparatively speaking, they experienced almost a golden age. Starting in A.D. 711, Muhammad and his Islamic (Muslim) followers, most of them dark-skinned North African Moors, had taken control of several parts of the world, including Spain. They permitted the Sephardic Spanish-speaking Jews[6] to work in most trades and professions. Many had brethren in faraway lands and were able to establish trading businesses, bringing in silks, spices, and other luxuries from distant places.

In 1391 a tidal wave of violence against both Jews and Muslims swept across the major Spanish city-states of Castile and Aragon. The Muslims and Jews were offered the chance to convert to Christianity or lose their lives. Most of them, of course, chose life. They became *conversos* (new Christians, or converts), but for obvious reasons the ruling Christians did not trust their sincerity. They labeled the Jewish converts *marranos* (pigs) and the Muslim converts *mariscos* (fish).

The Jews who refused to abandon their religion were forced into walled ghettos to prevent them from associating with the new Christians. They were excluded from the craft guilds and left to survive as best they could. Most of the Muslims went home to North Africa, but the Jews had no other homeland.

When two powerful monarchs, Isabella and Ferdinand, married in 1469, they launched and won a "just and holy war," later known as the Reconquista, to unite their kingdoms under the Catholic banner. As thousands of *conversos* were executed or fled for their lives, the church officials who ran the Spanish Inquisition took their property. This theft by murder became so obvious that even the Pope spoke out against the "love of lucre" of the inquisitors.[7] Granada, the last area of Islamic rule, surrendered on January 2, 1492. Meanwhile, Columbus was busy expanding Isabella and Ferdinand's realm on distant shores.

On March 31, 1492, all Jews were ordered to leave Spain within four months.[8] Between 50,000 and 100,000 Jews fled, scattering to wherever they had business contacts, friends, or relatives. Some of them were offered a chance to migrate to sparsely settled and dangerous colonies like Brazil, Jamaica, Curaçao, and Barbados, where a few Sephardim built up trading businesses in sugar, tobacco, cotton, and indigo.

Jews were allowed to settle in Amsterdam, the Dutch capi-

Seventeenth-century Jewish quarter of Amsterdam

tal, because of a raging feud between Dutch Protestants and Spanish Catholics. When the Dutch acquired a portion of Brazil's huge expanse in 1630, they offered Amsterdam Jews a chance to settle there. Their welcome lasted less than twenty-five years. In 1654, the Portuguese conquered Brazil for the second time and the Sephardic Jews were on the run again, heading for other Dutch colonies in the Caribbean.

Twenty-three Sephardim never reached their destination.[9] They were soon to be America's first Jewish inhabitants.

Spanish pirates captured their ship, but the twenty-three were miraculously rescued by a better-armed French merchant ship. After they turned over most of their money to the ship's captain, he dropped them off at his first stop, New Amsterdam, present-day New York City—then a primitive outpost of the Dutch West Indies Trading Company.

The stranded Jews immediately were made to feel most unwelcome. The captain of the French ship demanded more money, but the refugees were out of cash. The local authorities ordered their possessions sold at auction and jailed two of them until the "ransom" was sent by relatives abroad.

Even worse, Peter Stuyvesant, the one-legged Dutch governor, who firmly believed that Jews were "Christ killers" and thieves, ordered them expelled. The Jews managed to send a message by ship to friends in Holland. A special petition from Jewish stockholders persuaded the Dutch West Indies Company to order Stuyvesant to grant the Jews sanctuary.

The Sephardim stayed, but Stuyvesant had his revenge. He banned his new guests from praying in public, owning property, working at most jobs, employing Christians, and traveling without permission. Jews were not even permitted to join the Citizens Guards to defend themselves against Indian attacks![10] Asser Levy, a butcher by trade, organized a protest, and a year later Stuyvesant was forced to grant the Jews full citizenship rights.

In 1664 the English captured New Amsterdam and renamed it New York after the brother of King Charles II, the duke of York. Life for the Jews didn't change much. By 1695 about 3,500 people lived in New York, including twenty Jewish families. By then the tiny Jewish enclave included a handful of German and Polish Jews called Ashkenazim. The Sephardim and Ashkenazim had little to do with one another and did not even speak the same language: the Ashkenazim spoke Yiddish, a German-Polish dialect, and were considerably poorer than the Sephardim; many of them had escaped persecution in Poland with nothing but their lives.[11]

By the middle of the eighteenth century, Jews in the United States were still few in number. New York City, Newport, Rhode Island, and Charleston, South Carolina, were developing as important colonial seaports. There were few shops then, and most people purchased their cotton goods, tools, and trinkets from peddlers. Soon Jewish peddlers joined Yankee peddlers plying their wares throughout the colonies.

This was a time of unusual peace for the Jewish colonists. Although laws were occasionally passed depriving Jews of privileges such as voting rights, they were usually repealed when pressure was applied.[12] To become more socially acceptable, some Sephardim converted and intermarried with non-Jews. The more religious Ashkenazim were less willing to integrate and sometimes caused conflicts. In 1733, for example, forty-two Ashkenazi German and Sephardic Spanish-Portuguese Jews were sent to a new British colony in Georgia. The German Jews wanted to open a synagogue, but the Sephardim blocked their petitions for many months, undoubtedly believing that they would do better if they weren't "too Jewish."[13]

When Georgia failed to prosper, many of the Sephardic Jewish settlers left for Charleston, South Carolina, and built up trading businesses there. In Charleston a more liberal atmosphere prevailed. Skilled merchants were assets to the community, able to bring in much-wanted goods, including slaves.

Harold Isaacs, in an article that appeared in the *New Yorker* on May 13, 1961, said that he "had the small but consoling thought that my ancestors . . . were sequestered in some Eastern European ghetto and could not have been among the slavers who waited out there on those ships."[14] What Isaacs said was probably true about his particular ancestors. The vast majority of Russian Jews arrived in the United States at the end of the nineteenth century and early in the twentieth, when slavery was a thing of the past. But if he was referring to all Jews, he was mistaken. With the exception of the Quakers, most prosperous businesspeople and planters in the colonies, better-off Jews included, bought and sold slaves. A few were even part of the infamous industry of slave shipping.[15]

Although Jews were undoubtedly the least popular colonists, no one threatened to expel them. There were plenty of other available scapegoats. The African slaves were the "other" in the New World, forsaken by everyone, their families broken up, each slave alone, abandoned, and abused.[16]

Sheltered in crowded shanties with no sanitation, surviving on a meager diet of cornmeal and fatback, the kidnapped African slaves were lucky to stay alive. In some places as many as one-quarter of them died during their first few months of captivity. Resistance was rarely successful. Rigidly enforced laws meant torture, mutilation, and even death for any sign of disobedience.[17] Many ran away, some hoping to find their families. Others stole food, worked as slowly as possible, broke tools, and sabotaged crops, playing dumb for the overseers.

If African slaves had white friends at all in the colonies, they were found among a group of near slaves called indentured servants. Eager for new opportunities, thousands of impoverished Europeans, unable to pay for their passage, indebted themselves to ship captains and labor agents as indentured workers for five to seven years.[18]

Colonial society's economic structure resembled a five-layer wedding cake. On the top were the wealthy landowners and merchants; in the middle, their comfortable managers; below them, the free white workers and tenant farmers who were always on the edge of poverty; next came the indentured servants; and on the very bottom was a large layer representing the slaves, creating wealth for the top two layers with no compensation.

The population of the colonies grew from 250,000 in 1700 to 1,600,000 in 1760. The housing and food needs of the swelling population often were not met. As early as 1713 hungry crowds broke into warehouses loaded with grain for shipment overseas.[19] Cities were filled with homeless people including the aged as well as recent immigrants, and children. Every city had poorhouses, miserable and dangerous places much like the shelters for the homeless today.[20]

In many areas, poor farmers occupied land and refused to pay rent.[21] Just as impoverished workers were characterized as lowlifes, rebellious farmers were seen as "the dregs of the People."[22] But if their leaders were imprisoned, it was not unusual for crowds to break down the jail door and release them.

By the middle decades of the eighteenth century, the colonies were ready to explode. Throughout world history, the top layers, when threatened, often used wars to disperse the anger of the bottom layers. Soon the American Revolution against British rule would quiet down the anger about the lack of equality in the colonies.

The issue of impressment (forced service) in the British navy had cropped up in Boston in the 1730s and 1740s. Wealthy merchants, profiting from increased sales during England's many wars, had condemned the demonstrators as a "Riotous Tumultuous Assembly of Foreign Seamen, Servants, Negroes, and other Persons of Mean and Vile Condition."[23] By the late 1760s, as British taxes increased, the merchants, a handful of Jews included, developed an increased yearning for freedom from British control. The time seemed ripe for rebellion. The working people were angry because British troops stationed in several cities were permitted to take jobs in their off hours while colonial workmen went unemployed. Boston, where many British soldiers were working, became the starting point of the American Revolution. On March 5, 1770, ropemakers demonstrated on the jobs issue, and some of the soldiers lost control and fired into the crowd. Five men lost their lives in this famous incident, known as the Boston Massacre. The first man to fall was a black seaman named Crispus Attucks, a runaway slave.[24]

As much as the elite wanted freedom from British control, they were concerned that the majority of the citizenry would turn them out along with their British overseers. They turned to popular middle-class intellectuals who had often sided with the farmers and workers, counting on them to control the "rabble" and keep their anger focused on the British. As one historian expressed it, "the language of liberty and equality united just enough whites to fight a revolution against England, without ending either slavery or inequality."[25]

Not all of the colonists, of course, forgot their grievances against the colonial elite. Only about a third of the people actively supported the War for Independence. The rest were opposed to it or remained neutral. Alexander Hamilton, perhaps trying to shame men into fighting, said that his fellow colonists had "the passiveness of the sheep" and were "determined not to be free."[26]

The pronouncement of the Declaration of Independence

in July 1776 that "All men are created equal" carried the promise of a government representing everyone, but some people were aware that most of the signers of the declaration were wealthy planters, merchants, or lawyers. A committee during elections for a 1776 convention in Philadelphia, for example, submitted a bill of rights and urged voters to block the election of "great and overgrown rich men."[27]

Having learned that a call for the abolition of slavery had not been included in the Declaration of Independence, a group of Connecticut slaves managed to smuggle a statement of protest to the Founding Fathers. In Massachusetts a few legislators presented an antislavery bill to John Adams, the Massachusetts delegate to the Continental Congress. Concerned about southern participation in the Revolution, Adams expressed the hope that "The bill for freeing the Negroes ... will sleep for a time."[28] The time turned out to be about a century.

A few days after the Declaration of Independence was issued, a military draft was announced. In Massachusetts, draft-eligible men were permitted to hire substitutes. Obviously, this meant that the poor would fight the war. Rioters in the streets shouted, "Tyranny is tyranny let it come from whom it may."[29] As men who had bought their way out of service grew rich from war profits, the men in the battlefields watched their comrades die. Some rebelled against their officers.[30]

Jewish merchants generally supported the Revolution, eager for liberty from British taxes and controls. In both the northern and the southern colonies, many poorer Jews, believing in the Declaration of Independence, took their place in the Continental Army. In South Carolina, for example, Captain Richard Lushington headed up a "Jews' Army," a contingent that included many Jews from Charleston. As would happen again during the Civil War, some Jewish families, like the Franks family of Philadelphia, split over the issue of war against England.[31] A few well-off Jews played an important role in financing the Revolution.

The attitude toward the War for Independence of both free and enslaved African Americans was directly tied to their hope for liberation. In the first battles of the war, the names of several heroic black Minutemen were recorded: Peter Salem, Cato Stedman, Cuff Whittemore, Cato Wood, Lemuel Haynes, Pomp Blackman, and many others.[32]

James Madison and Alexander Hamilton urged slaves to enlist and win their freedom. African men, enslaved and free, participated in most of the major battles.[33]

Slave owners objected to black men fighting, fearing the impact it would have on their slaves. On November 12, 1775, Washington ordered recruiting stations to reject "Negroes, boys unable to bear arms, or old men unable to endure the fatigues of campaign."[34] The British governor of Virginia, Lord Dunmore, immediately announced that the British were willing to recruit black men. Washington then offered slaves a new deal. They could join up if their owners consented. At the end of the war they would be freed and given fifty dollars. Their former owners would be paid a thousand. Only a few slave owners in Maryland took Washington up on his offer.

Of three hundred thousand soldiers who served in the Continental Army, about five thousand were free black men from the North. Some served in segregated units and some were integrated into white units, although some generals protested.[35]

By June 1779, the British were suffering many defeats. Sir Henry Clinton, commander of the British forces, announced that any captured black man in the Continental Army would be sold into slavery but that those who deserted to the British lines would be freed. Freedom was freedom, no matter the color of a white man's uniform, and hundreds of runaway slaves accepted Clinton's invitation.

In June 1780, Charleston, South Carolina, fell to the British. Squads of black soldiers were sent to capture the city's cannons. Black slaves slipped away and joined their brothers. About 50,000 slaves from South Carolina and Georgia joined the British troops.

With the victory of the Continental forces at Yorktown on September 19, 1781, the Loyalists (colonists who had supported the British) fled for their lives. In the South, slave owners rushed to retrieve their property before the freed slaves could escape on British ships or to the North. Thousands eluded them and resettled in England and several British colonies. Washington thought some of his own slaves might have gone with them.

The vast majority of black people remained in bondage, however. Those who remained in the North as free men and women hoped that they would be treated as though they had been created equal and that their brothers and sisters would soon be liberated.

The depth of this feeling was revealed in a composition written by a seven-year-old black schoolchild in Cincinnati. The assigned topic was "What do you think most about?" The child's answer:

> ... to get the poor slaves from bondage. And I am sorrow to hear that the boat ... went down with 200 poor slaves from up the river. Oh how sorrow I am to hear that, it grieves my heart so that I could faint in a minute.[36]

Chapter

IN THE LAND
OF THE FREE

In 1790 the first census of the newborn democracy reported that almost one-fifth of the population, three-quarters of a million people, lived under the yoke of slavery. For almost an entire century after the American Revolution, the slavery issue held center stage. As the United States acquired vast territories, debates over the question of whether the new areas would be slave or free echoed not only in the halls of Congress but in the homes and streets of America's cities.[1]

The issue of the wide gap between the haves and have-nots remained at the core of every problem. In the South, plantation owners reaped in riches from agricultural products produced by slave labor. In the North, new industrialists accumulated profits from the twelve- to fourteen-hour workdays of native-born and immigrant workers, including children.

In every group, however, there were some who refused to be victimized. In the dead of night, workers organized unions—women in the mills of New England, and Mexicans in the mines of Colorado. Strikes and land wars, urban riots, and protest meetings went on even before the ink was dry on the Constitution.[2] The salient issue for the fifty-nine thousand free African Americans was freeing "the poor slaves from bondage." It was from among this group that the battle to end slavery found its earliest and most courageous leaders.[3]

One of the first, Quok Walker, a Massachusetts ex-slave, escaped during the confusion of the American Revolution but was found by his master and severely beaten. Walker went to court and sued for his freedom under a provision of the new

Massachusetts state constitution which stated that men were born free. Walker fought his case right up to the Massachusetts Supreme Court and won. His personal crusade guaranteed that slavery would no longer be permitted in the state of Massachusetts.

But Massachusetts was only one state. African Americans and their supporters hoped that the men attending the Constitutional Convention in 1787 would end the "peculiar institution" nationally. But as they framed the new Constitution, little was said on behalf of more than half a million slaves. States' rights were guaranteed, which meant that slavery would continue. Slave-ship owners would be permitted to continue their hellish journeys for another twenty years, dumping at least three million more people from Africa into the wretched slave quarters of the South. Even in the North, slavery was outlawed slowly, state by state. In 1810 there were still thirty thousand slaves in the North, a quarter of the black population; in 1840, still a thousand.

Arming themselves with homemade weapons, some slaves fought back. They preferred almost certain death to continued bondage. In 1800, Gabriel Prosser and a thousand slaves marched on the city of Richmond. In 1822, near Charleston, South Carolina, Denmark Vesey gathered an amazing nine thousand followers and plotted a rebellion. In 1831, Nat Turner and his followers stormed over a large area of Virginia, liberating slaves and killing their masters as they went. They struck terror in the hearts of the slave owners, but their rebellions always ended in defeat and gruesome death for the brave rebels.

The newly organized United States militia and army pointedly excluded "blacks, mulattoes and Indians," as though the darker-skinned heroes of the Revolution had never existed.[4] During the War of 1812, when the British attempted to regain their naval control over the United States, black men offered to fight, believing that military service would put them on the road to equality. Most were turned away until naval commanders, desperate when casualties depleted their crews, lifted the color ban. In the Great Lakes, at least one-tenth of Commander Oliver H. Perry's integrated crews were African Americans. After the war, Perry had nothing but praise for the black sailors.

But it was in New Orleans that black troops made the most significant difference between defeat and victory. General Andrew Jackson, who later would be president, knew that defeat was imminent as a fleet of British ships stormed into the port, ready to capture the city. Back in 1804 some fifty-five black Revolutionary War veterans had won the right to form a Mulatto Corps. Jackson called for free African American volunteers to join this nucleus, offering them "the same bounty in money and lands now received by white soldiers" as well as equal pay and conditions. Hundreds of blacks responded and helped save New Orleans in 1814.

"The President . . . shall hear," Jackson promised them, "how praiseworthy was your conduct in the hour of danger."[5] Five years after Jackson made his promises, all "Negroes or mulattoes" were once again barred from military service. In 1828, Jackson ran for president. The hopes of foes of slavery died when Jackson, himself a Tennessee plantation owner, chose John C. Calhoun, a senator from South Carolina and a leading advocate of slavery, as his running mate.

Some men of African heritage, like Paul Cuffee of Massachusetts, a successful black businessman, gave up the struggle to find equality in the United States and funded a back-to-Africa movement. Financing the plan himself, Cuffee took thirty-eight black people on his ship and sailed for Sierra Leone.

From the opposite point of view, another back-to-Africa movement was attempted by a group of prominent slaveholders. Realizing that free African Americans would never give up the struggle until slavery was abolished, they decided it was best to remove these potential troublemakers. They organized the American Colonization Society and persuaded Congress to appropriate funds for land in Africa. In twenty years they found few takers for the new colony in Liberia, and the plan petered out by 1840. For most African Americans, the United States was their birthplace and Africa was a little known, distant continent. They wanted to make a stand for freedom in the country they had shed blood to help create.

No compromise was possible for the people who were devoting their time, and in some cases, their lives, to the antislavery cause. In 1828, David Walker, an African American shopkeeper in Boston, returned horrified after a trip through the slave South. He issued an "Appeal to the Colored Citizens of the World," urging slaves "to kill or be killed." Black sailors helped Walker smuggle his appeal into the slave states. Southern militiamen ransacked ships searching for Walker's pamphlet, and new laws were quickly passed decreeing the death sentence for anyone distributing it. In Boston, friends warned Walker that a group of well-off southerners was offering three thousand dollars to anyone who murdered him. They urged Walker to flee to Canada. Walker refused to leave. "Somebody must die in this cause," he said.[6] A year later David Walker died under mysterious circumstances.

Over the next decades, ex-slaves like Harriet Tubman, Sojourner Truth, and Frederick Douglass took to the roads, sharing speakers' platforms with white abolitionists like Wendell Phillips of Boston and a Quaker woman named Lucretia Mott. Hundreds of antislavery leaflets and books were printed and distributed in a battle "fought largely with words."[7]

David Walker had called for slave revolts, and later John Brown would do the same, but most abolitionists remained opposed to violence in any form. Some of them changed their minds as the racist propaganda of the slaveholders inspired violence against people of African descent all over the nation.

Underpaid or jobless whites, instead of protesting against the men who kept them impoverished, often turned their anger against African Americans, driving them out of their homes and burning their neighborhoods to the ground so that they could not return. In 1829 mob violence forced more than half of the free black population of Cincinnati to flee the city. Five years later hundreds of others were driven out of Philadelphia. Canada was often the closest safe place for endangered African Americans. Ohio and Illinois required every new black settler to post a bond of $500 to $1,000. Indiana excluded black people completely, even those who had money. The Westward Ho movement had a whites-only provision. Just about every state prohibited blacks from voting, owning property, serving on juries, and joining the state militia. Even the U.S. Post Office refused to hire African Americans.

While slaves ate their cornmeal and salt pork rations, their masters feasted on the chickens the slaves had raised and the fruits and vegetables they had planted, weeded, and harvested. While slave owners lived in palatial plantation mansions, the people who had helped build them lived in windowless, mud-floored, cabins. Grief stalked the daily lives of America's slaves. Family members were separated, sold off with the stroke of a pen, as mothers wept. Epidemics were frequent and deadly, but only the wealthiest planters saw to it that doctors visited the slave quarters. Some white physicians offered discounts if they could use slaves as medical guinea pigs to improve their techniques.

Dr. J. Marion Sims, for example, is often cited as the "father of gynecology." He tested his surgical theories by performing dozens of operations on a slave woman named Anarcha in the 1840s. By 1853, sure of his talents, he started a highly lucrative practice in New York City and went on to become chief surgeon at New York Woman's Hospital.[8]

Escape became the favorite form of resistance. Some slaves ran away on foot and hid out in forests and swamps, evading bloodhounds and slave catchers. A slave named Henry Brown sealed himself into a box, and friends shipped him to Philadelphia. Frederick Douglass used forged papers to make his way north. Harriet Tubman hiked by night from Maryland to Pennsylvania.

The 1840s through 1860s have been called the Age of Reform.[9] By 1842, there were two thousand state and local anti-slavery groups with about 200,000 members. All over the country, Americans who believed that "all men are created equal" organized the Underground Railroad, a network of people ready to hide and protect fugitive slaves on their long trip to the North. The "conductors," many of whom were former slaves themselves, led the fugitives to the attics and basements of white and black storekeepers, merchants, and farmers.

Runaway slaves soon discovered that stories of a free life in the North bore little resemblance to the reality, however. Black men were the last to be hired and the first to be fired even from the most menial jobs. Hospitals turned black patients away, and it was not until 1841 that a few beds in Bellevue Hospital in New York City were set aside for "colored" patients.

After long struggles, a few segregated schools were opened, but often they were housed in a basement or an old shack. Even private schools were reluctant to admit those rare African American children whose parents could afford the tuition. Noyes Academy in Canaan, New Hampshire, quietly enrolled fourteen black children in 1835. In retaliation, town citizens gathered a herd of one hundred oxen, attached the animals to the school building, and pulled it off its foundations.[10] Most restaurants, trains, and places of entertainment barred African Americans or set aside separate inferior facilities for them. Frederick Douglass introduced the form of resistance that would later be called "civil disobedience." He would stay in a restaurant, occupying a seat without being served, until he was forced to leave. Congress passed the Fugitive Slave Act of 1850, stipulating that any free African American, North or South, could be grabbed and declared a slave *with no proof required!* This proved to be the last straw. Some African Americans emigrated to Canada. Others formed self-defense committees, taking Frederick Douglass's advice that "Every colored man in the country should sleep with his revolver under his head, loaded and ready for use."[11]

The abolitionist movement grew. In several places townspeople stormed jails to free captured black men. Sometimes the crowds numbered in the thousands. Ignoring public opinion, the federal government continued to refuse to rescind the Fugitive Slave Act. In 1857 the Supreme Court handed down a decision in the Dred Scott case that further heated up the situation. Scott, a slave who had been taken by his owner to a free state, argued that his status had changed to that of a free man. Not so, the Court ruled. Blacks were not citizens and therefore had no rights. The antislavery movement moved into still higher gear.

Two years later, John Brown, a white soldier, and a small band of his supporters in Kansas made plans to invade the South and inspire a slave revolt. Frederick Douglass, certain that the plan would fail, tried to persuade Brown to abandon it. Brown and his twenty-one Raiders—including seven blacks and three Jews—captured the government arsenal at Harpers Ferry, West Virginia, in order to seize arms. The marines came with full firepower, captured the survivors, and charged them with treason. Brown and six of his comrades were sentenced to hang, but their motives and courage did not go unnoticed. Ralph Waldo Emerson called Brown "that new saint who will make the gallows as glorious as the cross."[12]

America's Jews were divided on the slavery issue both before and during the Civil War. By 1850, when the Fugitive Slave Act was passed, there were only about 50,000 Jews, spread all over the country. A decade later their numbers had tripled to 150,000. Most of the recent immigrants knew little about the controversy. They were trying to adjust to a new homeland and a new language.

Antislavery leaders knew that Jews had been persecuted and expected them to become activists. In its thirteenth annual report in 1853, the American and Foreign Anti-Slavery Society commented:

> *The objects of so much mean prejudice and unrighteous oppression as the Jews have been for ages, surely they, it would seem, more than any other denomination, ought to be the enemies of* caste, *and the friends of universal freedom.*[13]

Actually, it would have been impossible for any denominational opinion to be promulgated in the name of all Jews. There was no single spokesperson for American Jewry. Language and religious differences made it difficult to create one ruling body. Forgotten in the frenzy of antiblack racism, Jews had not been too often attacked. Most of them thought it best to keep their mouths shut on the burning issues of the day. The anti-Semitism in the culture of the new nation was scary. Across America, new versions of the caricatured "Jewish villain" of British plays emerged in popular skits. Several best-selling novels featured similarly hideous characters.[14] Although a number of writers took issue with this portrayal, their essays seldom reached the public who followed the popular press and theater.[15]

Most of the handful of early Jewish Americans must have felt lucky to have white skin. If they were careful they could have a decent life in the newborn nation. Long before the Civil

War, a few Jews were working for the government as port officers, Indian agents, even American consular agents. In New York City, the powerful political Tammany Society, which dispensed jobs to new arrivals, elected a Jewish president, Solomon Simson, in 1797. From 1802 until his retirement in 1844, the head of New York City's day police force was a Jew named Jacob Hays, famous as an almost single-handed law enforcer in the population of 65,000.[16]

Jewish men were free to join the army, navy, and militia, and many fought in the War of 1812. Uriah P. Levy, a navy man, claimed that he was "slighted, rebuffed, and discriminated against during most of his career . . . and in 1855 . . . a board sought to purge him from the navy." But despite his complaints, Levy was promoted to the highest naval rank of commodore.[17] Under his command, corporal punishment in the navy was abolished.

Only a few of the German Jewish immigrants who arrived during the pre-Civil War period were politically inclined, having been involved in the German democratic revolution of 1848 and having fled after its failure. Most came because the German economy was experiencing a sharp decline. They arrived with some money to invest and moved from peddling to setting up neighborhood stores in new settlements all over the country.

Most did not convert to Christianity, but many practiced a modernized version of the Jewish religion, known as Reform Judaism. They cut off their long sideburns, changed from frock coats and top hats into Yankee clothing, and studied English. Orthodox women removed their wigs and let their hair tumble out. All of these "reforms" made it easier for them to function in the new nation.

The bulk of the world's socially conscious Jewish activists, who might have been likelier recruits for the antislavery movement, were stuck in czarist Russia, persecuted and too poor to pay for their passage to America. They would not arrive in the United States until the close of the nineteenth century and the early years of the twentieth, well after the end of the Civil War.

Jews in the South numbered a tiny minority of 15,000 among 9 million southern whites. In public they behaved like most Christians. Jewish and Christian slave owners continued to buy and sell slaves. Those who opposed slavery expressed their opposition in private.[18] In the North, a few Jews took a firm stand on the slavery issue. Three young recently arrived Jewish men were among John Brown's Raiders: Theodore Weiner from Poland, Jacob Benjamin from Bohemia, and August Bondi from Vienna. A New York merchant, Moses Judah, was an active member of the New York Manumission Society, working to persuade slaveowners to release their slaves. Several Philadelphia Jews were members of a local abolitionist society. Bavarian born Louis Stix, a peddler with large territories in the South, risked his life to oppose slavery. Later he said, it "cost me the goodwill of many Southern customers, and at no time before the war was it considered safe for me to venture south of the Mason and Dixon's [sic] line."[19]

In New York, Rabbi Morris Jacob Raphall sermonized on the scriptural justifications for slavery, while Dr. David Einhorn, the rabbi of a synagogue in Baltimore, Maryland, a slave city in a slave state, agitated so powerfully against it that in 1851 he was forced to flee.[20] Ernestine Rose, the daughter of a Polish rabbi, joined the abolitionist movement soon after her arrival in this country in 1836 and made speeches all over the country.

Many German Jews were not eager to befriend these *Outlaws in the Promised Land*, however. They had decided that if they learned English and became as non-Jewish as possible, they could escape the most overt anti-Semitism.

With the outbreak of the Civil War, regional loyalties generally determined who fought on the side of the Union and who joined the Confederacy. Estimates of Jewish men fighting in the war range from 8,000 to 20,000. About four times as many Jews fought with Union forces as with the Confederacy. In New York alone, more than 2,000 Jews joined the Union Army. Many became officers, and several won the Congressional Medal of Honor.[21]

Because European leaders believed the Confederacy would win, it was difficult for the Union to obtain loans. General Ulysses S. Grant turned to a Jewish friend, Jessie Seligman, who had run a small clothing store near West Point when Grant was stationed there. Seligman had family banking connections in Europe, and he and his brothers sold 200 million dollars' worth of Union bonds.[22]

There is no record of the Seligmans' reaction in 1862, when Grant issued General Order No. 11, calling for all Jews "as a class" to be expelled from his Tennessee command area within twenty-four hours or face arrest and imprisonment with no right to appeal. There had been heavy cotton speculating and smuggling in the area, and although some Jews were involved, they were vastly outnumbered by Christian traders, among them Grant's own father, whom Grant allowed to remain. Jewish men, women, and children—whether or not they had ever traded with the enemy—were rounded up and shipped out. When one of them asked the reason, he received the eternal answer: "Because you are Jews."[23]

Protest letters poured into the White House and President Abraham Lincoln soon had the expulsion order canceled. Still, offering one's life and limb as well as one's purse had obviously not eradicated anti-Semitism.

African Americans, of course, had no stake in fighting for the Confederacy, but for many months they were excluded from serving in the Union army because Lincoln feared that the border states would join the Confederacy if black men were armed. Urged by Frederick Douglass and other abolitionist leaders to change this policy, Lincoln continued to refuse. But by late 1862, volunteering slowed almost to a halt as word came of Union defeats. The Conscription Act of 1863 once again allowed the rich to buy their way out of service. Many poor whites resented this and believed the war was being fought for black liberation, an issue that didn't particularly concern most of them. During draft riots in several northern cities, homes and businesses owned by African Americans were burned to the ground and any black person in the area was in danger of attack.[24]

If the Union was to win the war, the only answer for Lincoln was to change his policy. His Emancipation Proclamation freed the slaves, and close to 200,000 black men served in Union forces during the remainder of the Civil War, about half of them bearing arms.[25]

At war's end, thousands of blacks celebrated their new-found freedom, but when the parties were over, the harsh reality set in. Newly freed slaves, most of them without shelter, food, or medical care, wandered the war-torn South, searching for lost families, work, food, and shelter. Almost half were school-age children.

Federal troops were stationed in the South to protect the newly freed slaves. The federal government established the Freedmen's Bureau in March 1865 to handle the staggering resettlement problem. The nation's first Civil Rights Act was signed into law the following year, guaranteeing everyone except Indians and women equality before the law. Congress, voting to provide every former slave with forty acres and a mule, also appropriated money for freedmen's schools and hospitals. African American and white teachers, doctors, and nurses journeyed south to help. Day schools, night schools, teachers' training schools, and prestigious colleges such as Howard University opened their doors to blacks. For African Americans these Reconstruction programs offered great hope. Black men were elected to state legislatures and even to Congress. It is interesting to note that American women of all races continued to be denied the vote for another half century, however.

A decade later the bright dreams and hopes of Reconstruction faded. The Freedmen's Bureau had never received enough land to provide each ex-slave family with even one acre, let alone forty. President Andrew Johnson issued pardons to the Confederates, and they reclaimed their confiscated lands. A few promising new black settlements were broken up, and the owners were told to work as contracted laborers before their first crops were even harvested.[26]

King Dollar quickly won the battle over Queen Morality. As war profits disappeared, the economy went into a tailspin. Congress decided to balance the budget by closing down the Freedmen's Bureau. Federal troops were pulled out of the South.

As soon as the soldiers left, an orgy of revenge was born. Black Codes, laws segregating whites from blacks in all public facilities, were swiftly enacted. Rigid literacy tests and property ownership requirements disenfranchised African Americans.

Anyone who protested became a target of the newly empowered Ku Klux Klan, gangs of white-hooded men who rode in the night to murder blacks and those who supported them.[27] In 1883, as a virtual reign of terror gripped the South, the Supreme Court nullified the Civil Rights Act. In 1896, in *Plessy* v. *Ferguson*, the Court ruled that "separate but equal" facilities were constitutional. Segregation now had the official stamp of approval.

The frontier was pushed westward, railroad tracks spread like spiderwebs over the nation, overseas possessions and spheres of influence expanded, and factory smokestacks became a common part of the landscape as the United States rapidly became a leading world industrial power. For Native Americans, the new frontier brought death or confinement to reservations. Mexican Americans remained the primary target of racists throughout the Southwest as they dug out the copper, picked the cotton, and held the worst-paying jobs.[28] Japanese and Chinese workers were brought by the boatload to lay railroad tracks in the hot sun and then shipped back home with next to nothing in their pockets. Cubans, Puerto Ricans, and Filipinos hoped that American troops would help free them from the yoke of Spanish colonialism only to find themselves under the control of American planters.

Immigrant workers—Jews and Italians in garment sweatshops and Slovaks in Pittsburgh steel mills[29]—worked grueling twelve-hour days. Even worse they saw their children, many of them no older than eight, enter the same plant gates unprotected by child labor laws for many years.

Few would dispute the fact, however, that the members of the largest single minority group, African Americans, were—and still are—the worst off,[30] virtually excluded from most areas of American life. The bulk of the black population stayed in the South until the first decades of the twentieth century, moving from one rural area to another or drifting into cities and towns.

Chapter *three*

BLACKS AND JEWS—UNWELCOME NEW YORKERS

An enduring myth, no truer than the Santa Claus story, surrounds the arrival of waves of immigrants from all over Europe between the 1880s and the 1920s. It goes something like this: A shipload of immigrants arrives in New York Harbor. Hundreds of passengers cheer as they spot the upraised arm of the "Mother of Exiles," the Statue of Liberty. Most of the weary travelers cannot speak or read English, but they know the meaning of the lines inscribed on the statue's pedestal: "Give me your tired, your poor . . . The wretched refuse of your teeming shore. . . . I lift my lamp beside the golden door."

The story is false on several scores. The famous poem "The New Colossus," written by a Sephardic Jew named Emma Lazarus, was placed out of sight on an interior wall of the pedestal of the Statue of Liberty in 1903. In 1924 harsh immigration laws closed the "golden door" most of the way, leaving only a thin crack for a few immigrants who were able to slip in under rigid quotas favoring white Protestants. In the 1930s and throughout World War II, hardly any of the victims of Nazi persecution were permitted to come into the protective embrace of the Mother of Exiles. The tablet containing the poem was not placed over the entranceway to the Statue until 1945, after more than six million Jews had been slaughtered in Nazi concentration camps.[1]

In the 1870s, before the statue was brought to New York Harbor, about 40,000 Jewish immigrants from Eastern Europe trickled in.[2] Most of them were middle class or at least skilled tradesmen. They spread out into German Jewish communities in many parts of the nation, blending in nicely. It would be another couple of decades before millions of "huddled masses" arrived.

Most people are reluctant to leave the country of their birth to travel to a faraway land where strangers speak an unfamiliar language and there is seldom a warm reception. Like the Sephardic Jews of Spain, Eastern European Jews stayed put until they were desperate.

But unlike the Sephardic Jews, the Jews of Russia and Poland never enjoyed a period of prosperity.[3] Catherine the Great, empress of Russia, barred Jews from her country. In 1795, when Poland was divided up and Russia grabbed off the largest chunk of it, almost one million Jews were included in the package. The "enlightened" Catherine set aside a special area for Jews, later known as the Pale of Settlement, where they were isolated in Yiddish-speaking communities called shtetls.

Under a succession of czars, Jews were watched closely. Dozens of laws banned them from travel and from most occupations. To survive, they peddled their produce and services to one another and to the local peasants and hired themselves out as wage laborers, working at the dirtiest and worst jobs, "fit only for a Jew"—(pretty much the same jobs reserved in the United States for free blacks). Life revolved around survival and prayer.

Jews were happily barred from the Russian army until 1827, when Czar Nicholas I changed the rules. After that, a quota of Jewish boys was sent at age twelve to military schools. At eighteen the boys began twenty-five years of army service, and most of them never saw their families again. Local Jewish councils known as *kahals* were assigned the task of selecting the draftees, but they were disbanded when it was discovered that some of the members accepted bribes to spare the sons of better-off families. By 1844, the communities were run by self-help organizations, which one author called the "forerunners of Jewish trade unions."[4]

In the 1850s the Haskalah, the Jewish Enlightenment, made its way to Russia, spreading even to the isolated Orthodox schtetls. Some daring young men furtively read Enlightenment pamphlets and decided to abandon their Orthodox practices and join the Bund, the illegal General Jewish Workers' Union, hoping to establish a democratic socialist government.

Alexander II took over in 1855, and emancipated the serfs. Although they were now legally free, their tables were no fuller. Fearing a rebellion, Alexander II convinced the peasants that the Jews were to blame for their poverty. A paramilitary goon squad called the Black Hundreds, like the Ku Klux Klan in America, launched surprise raids called pogroms on the shtetls. Homes were burned down, the scant possessions of the Jewish residents were pillaged, women were raped, and always there were dead to be buried when the marauders left.[5]

In 1881 a small group called Narodniks, none of them Jewish and many of them anti-Semitic themselves, hoping to awaken the populace, assassinated the czar. Looking for a scapegoat, the government targeted not only Narodniks but also labor organizers and all Jews. The worst pogrom ever ensued and thousands of Jews fled. The Temporary Laws of May 31, 1882—the so-called May Laws—were passed, to "shield the Russian population against harmful Jewish activity."[6] Very similar to the Black Codes passed during the same period in the American South, the new edicts barred Jews from political life and sent them to work twelve-hour days in tobacco and garment factories at lower wages than those paid to Russian workers. Bund members worked secretly to improve working conditions, but they were frequently arrested. As the pogroms and hard times continued, hundreds of thousands of Russia's Jews saved their pennies and looked toward America.

Almost three-quarters of the new Jewish immigrants stayed where their ship landed—in New York City. Almost a million of them settled on the Lower East Side, and the rest overflowed into East Harlem[7] and into the Brooklyn communities of Williamsburg, Greenpoint, and Brownsville, making up 28 percent of the city's population.[8] By 1914 three million Jews lived in the United States, still only about 2.5 percent of the population.

Myths as persistent as the Statue of Liberty folktale have

claimed that these early immigrants were successful, but that is a far cry from the truth. Some of their children and grandchildren succeeded, but very few of the immigrants ever found the good life. Families and their boarders and relatives crowded into railroad flats in depressing tenements with one window at each end and a deep dark air shaft in the middle. Crawling and running vermin and rodents—roaches, bedbugs, and rats—were impossible to eliminate. People were everywhere, on stoops, on sidewalks, on fire escapes, and hanging out of windows. Noise, odors, and dirt seemed to replace air.

More than a third of the new arrivals found work in garment factories, where they were faced again with twelve-hour days and low wages. Others tried peddling without much success. The middle class shopped in stores opened by previous generations of peddlers, and the streets were overcrowded with men and women hawking their wares.

The Hebrew Sheltering and Immigrant Aid Society, sponsored by German Jews, helped the Russian Jews find temporary shelter, food, and clothing. "None were left to starve on docks."[9] But the Germans did not welcome their poor Yiddish-speaking brethren with open arms.[10] Most of them worried that the arrival of so many poorly dressed, Yiddish-speaking Orthodox Jews—or, even worse, radical Bundists—might cause a flare-up of anti-Semitism.

Most of the German Jews had been thoroughly Americanized by then. They had become garment manufacturers, businessmen, and professionals and had moved to spacious apartments on the Upper West Side of Manhattan. True, money could not buy full acceptance. The advertising brochures of some fashionable summer resorts and private schools contained words like "Churches close by" or, more explicitly, "No Hebrews wanted." Wealthier German Jews were able to build Jewish resorts, and newspapers listed their social activities along with those of German Christian clubs.[11] It was obvious to German Jews and other immigrant groups that becoming "Americanized" meant accepting the dominance of the white Anglo-Saxon Protestant (WASP) culture.

Some German Jewish organizations attempted to slow down the flow of immigrants. When that didn't work, they made a less than successful effort to disperse the newcomers to other cities and even to farm communities.[12] Prestigious Jewish magazines published many articles complaining about the new arrivals.[13]

Only a few observers noticed the many accomplishments of the "Downtown Jews," as the German Jews called them. Very little writing had emerged from the German Jewish communities. Americanization and success in business were not conducive to literary productivity. But in the tenements of New York City, novels and short stories were produced in English and in Yiddish; several daily and weekly Yiddish-language newspapers were born; and the Yiddish theater flourished. One enthusiastic admirer of the Eastern European immigrants commented that the Lower East Side was "pulsating with cultural life and creativity, peopled by men and women possessed of social concern and human sensitivity."[14]

Since there was no way to return the Eastern European Jews to Russia and its pogroms, the German Jewish organizations decided to Americanize them. In 1884, they financed the Hebrew Technical Institute for Jewish boys, a school that provided machine shop lessons, showers, lunches, and patriotic lectures. They also opened the Hebrew Institute, soon renamed the Educational Alliance, which offered free classes in many subjects as long as the students also attended English and Americanization classes.

Labor organizers on the Lower East Side, fearing that the conservative schools and settlement houses established by the German Jews would educate their children to become obedient workers, established the Educational League. Because it was underfunded, the league never enjoyed the success of the Educational Alliance.[15]

Embellishing the rags to riches myth is the often repeated story that immigrant Jewish children were pushed by their parents to study. The reality was that until the turn of the century the city had no centralized compulsory public school system, and there were almost no public high schools. The children of the wealthier classes attended private schools.[16]

About 20 percent of the Eastern European Jewish male immigrants and 40 percent of the women were illiterate. Their children went to work in factories as soon as they were tall enough to reach the machines, often by age eight. Early unions all during the nineteenth century had called for legislation for free public schools and the end of child labor, but business groups had steadfastedly resisted. As more and more immigrants arrived, Americanization became a major issue and the public school system suddenly expanded. Schools were soon overcrowded and even turned children away. Many left school and applied for their working papers when they were fourteen, with little hope of finding a decent job. In 1913, a report on New York City schools concluded that academic achievement on the Lower East Side had been poor.[17]

By the opening years of the twentieth century, plenty of jobs were available for public school teachers who had completed a short training period required at a public normal school. Many children of the poor took those jobs, but anti-Semitism made it difficult for any young Jewish teacher to land a permanent position. Many continued for years to work as low-paid substitutes. By 1911, women constituted 78 percent of all public school teachers. Since many of the teachers came from families with a strong union tradition, in 1916 the newly formed New York Teachers Union became the first group of public service workers to join the American Federation of Labor (AFL).

In accord with our layer-cake model, a pecking order in teacher training emerged: the poor became teachers in the public school system; those from better-off families trained in public college departments of education; from Columbia University Teachers' College, middle-class male students moved quickly into better paying administrative jobs.

The claim that the children of Eastern European Jewish immigrants became wealthy is not matched by evidence. In 1905, more than half of the young men and three-quarters of the young women were employed in manual trades. Most of the others in so-called nonmanual work were peddlers, small tradesmen, or low-paid clerks. Of the 12 percent of Jewish men categorized as entrepreneurs, many had invested in a few sewing machines, at fifty dollars each, and employed their own

*Hungarian immigrant family. In the late
nineteenth century, Jewish immigrants from
Eastern Europe were of a different class than
the German Jews who immigrated earlier.*

families and perhaps a boarder or two. By the 1920s, the majority of American Jews were still workers.

In many families, the daughters dropped out of school early to bring wages home. Perhaps one or two sons were able to attend tuition-free City College. The young women usually went to work in the garment shops. As one author said, it was "slaughter of the daughters to the glory of the sons."[18] The entire graduating class of CCNY numbered 209 in 1913, only 22 of them Jewish. It is true that by 1918–1919, some 78 percent of the students at CCNY and 38.7 percent at Hunter were from Jewish families, but percentages are deceptive. Actually, very few Jews went on to college.

For most Eastern European families, life continued to be a bitter struggle for survival. As the population swelled, social problems also increased. Terrible things happened in the packed Jewish neighborhoods that had never occurred in the Pale. Men deserted their families, young girls turned to prostitution, tuberculosis and other diseases raced through the tenements.

The *New York Tribune* published a description of the "foreign district" on November 25, 1900:

> *The big tenement houses in Chrystie Alley, Stanton and Forsyth Streets shelter crime in its worst form.... For years these places have been known by the [prostitutes'] red lamps which shone in the windows or hallways.*[19]

Concerned Jews often became socialists. The Socialist Labor Party, composed of about two thousand mainly non-Jewish German-speaking immigrants, fused with a small handful of Eastern European Jewish Bundists in the 1880s. In 1888 the party organized a union called United Hebrew Trades. In 1901 the Socialist Party of America was founded and soon became the nation's primary socialist group, with prominent Jewish labor leaders in its ranks.[20]

For two decades there were intermittent strikes in the garment sweatshops, many of them owned by German Jews. This immediately caused conflict between the uptown and downtown Jewish communities. The fear of unions interfering with business profits was certainly not a minor cause of the hostility of German Jews toward their Eastern European brethren.[21]

Most of the impoverished garment workers were willing to risk criticism from Uptown. Exclusion from expensive resorts had no impact on their lives, but wages and working conditions did. While Downtown Jews called manufacturers "exploiters" and were in turn called "dangerous anarchist socialists" by Uptown Jews,[22] in both groups there were some who wanted unity. But no joint organization emerged until labor strife between Jewish employers and workers became a national embarrassment.

Although about 90 percent of the workers in the garment lofts were young women, they received far lower wages than the men. They were the major participants in the "Uprising of the 20,000," an enormous strike in 1909–1910 that finally brought recognition for the International Ladies' Garment Workers' Union (ILGWU), but conditions improved only slightly.

On Saturday, March 26, 1911, a terrible fire broke out in the cramped headquarters of the Triangle Shirtwaist Company, occupying the top three floors of a loft building in Greenwich Village. The doors had been locked by management to prevent stealing, and the sewing machine operators could not escape. Fire hoses and ladders were unable to reach the blazing floors. One hundred forty-six employees, most of them young women, perished in the flames or jumped to their death.

A protest march of 50,000 people filled the streets of the Lower East Side after the tragedy. Rose Schneiderman, a young organizer for the ILGWU, traveled uptown to win the support of wealthy gentiles and Jews for the union. "I would be a traitor to those poor burned bodies if I came here to talk good fellowship," she told them. "We have tried you good people of the public and we have found you wanting," she began her speech at a rally at the Metropolitan Opera House on May 2, 1911.[23]

Meanwhile, anti-Semitism and anti-immigrant feelings were on the rise, fueled by a full-scale Americanization campaign in education and in the press. The New York Kehillah was quickly organized to combat anti-Semitism and coordinate educational and charity work among all New York Jews. In 1913 the Kehillah sent a German Jewish lawyer, Louis D. Brandeis, who later became the first Jewish Supreme Court justice, to negotiate a garment industry settlement called the Protocol of Peace. The settlement improved wages and working conditions, and by 1914 the ILGWU was the AFL's third largest union. In Chicago, another union, the Amalgamated Clothing Workers of America, grew out of the New York victory.

But then, in 1913, Leo Frank, the owner of a pencil factory in Atlanta, Georgia, was found guilty of the rape and murder of one of his factory workers, Mary Phagan, on what most later jurists believed was insufficient evidence. Frank was tried in the press long before the actual trial, and every Jewish stereotype was used against Frank. When the governor commuted Frank's death sentence to life imprisonment, a mob broke into the jail on August 6, 1915, and hanged Frank from a tree branch.[24]

Throughout the nation, enraged residents of Jewish communities organized and protested. Perhaps as compensation for the Frank lynching, in 1916, after a bitter struggle in the Senate for his confirmation, Louis D. Brandeis, was appointed to the Supreme Court by President Woodrow Wilson. That same year, Eastern European radical Jews attracted enough sympathizers to elect Meyer London, a socialist labor lawyer, to Congress. The most widely read Yiddish-language newspaper in the United States was the *Jewish Daily Forward*, edited by Abraham Cahan, another socialist.

While Leo Frank was one of the very few Jews lynched in the South, for African Americans lynching was a common event. Between 1885 and 1894, an estimated 1,700 black people died at the hands of lynch mobs. By the turn of the century these vigilante executions had at least doubled.[25]

Once again economics played a central role in the rise of racism. Agriculture had been severely damaged by the Civil War, and recovery was slow. White farmers, feeling threatened by cheap black labor, were the main supporters of a new Populist movement with racist undertones that gained strength in the early 1890s.[26]

Just as the Russian Jews had remained in their shtetls as long as possible, southern blacks tried to survive in the land of their fathers and mothers. A new generation of younger

African Americans understood the importance of forming their own organizations, but they also knew that any groups openly proclaiming a goal of equality were doomed to violent suppression. The black churches became extremely important, providing a safe haven where black men and women could meet.[27]

After Reconstruction, many northern businesses invested in southern railroads and textile mills but quickly let it be known that they preferred white workers. African Americans were permitted to apply for the leftover heaviest and lowest-paying jobs. As unions emerged, they also usually barred blacks.[28] Unions were weakened by their own racism. When workers struck, many employers turned to the vast army of starving unemployed, many of them black and Mexican, and hired them to replace striking workers.

Employers in the South found an even cheaper source of labor: convicts. Long lines of black men in striped uniforms, chained together at the ankles, using pickaxes to dig through rocks in quarries and repairing dams, became a common sight. Under the terms of a convict lease system, prisoners with long sentences or working off heavy fines were sent out to labor on chain gangs.

As the new century began, 95 percent of the nation's almost nine million African Americans still lived in the South. Black businesses were few, and only 2,500 African Americans had graduated from college, most of them from all-black institutions set up during Reconstruction.[29]

African American leaders differed sharply on solutions to the problems of black people. Over the next two decades, three major currents of thought were represented by Booker T. Washington's Tuskegee Institute, W. E. B. Du Bois's National Association for the Advancement of Colored People (NAACP), and later, Marcus Garvey's Universal Negro Improvement Association.[30]

Booker T. Washington focused his attention on the South, where he was born into slavery in 1856. Hired to run a training school for black teachers in Alabama, by 1881 he had used the labor and talent of his students to construct a real campus and a self-sustaining farm: Tuskegee Institute. In a speech at

Atlanta, Washington advised black people to stay in the rural South, concentrate on tilling the soil, and progress slowly. Struggling for equality, he believed, could lead only to bloodshed. Many powerful southern and northern whites responded by donating large sums of money to Tuskegee Institute. Julius Rosenwald, the son of a German Jewish peddler who went on to become a wealthy partner in Sears Roebuck in 1895, contributed the most, spending millions of dollars for the construction of schools for African American children in the South. Washington dined at the White House with Theodore Roosevelt and was awarded an honorary degree from Harvard University, where few black students were ever permitted to study.[31]

Some militant black leaders referred to Washington's Atlanta speech as "the Atlanta Compromise." When public schools for black children in South Carolina were threatened with closings during the heyday of the powerful Populist politician Ben Tillman, Washington's letter to Tillman further angered many black leaders. It said, in part,

> *I am but a humble member of an unfortunate race; you are a member of the great intelligent Caucasian race. ...I cannot believe that you ...are engaged in constructing laws that will keep 650,000 of my weak, dependent and unfortunate race in ignorance, poverty and crime.*[32]

William Edward Burghardt Du Bois was born in Massachusetts three years after the end of the Civil War and grew up as part of Boston's light-skinned mulatto elite of African Americans. In 1896, Du Bois, a sociologist, became one of the first African Americans to earn a Ph.D. from Harvard after it opened its doors to a few blacks.

Du Bois believed that Booker T. Washington's philosophy had helped to maintain the second-class status of blacks in the South and even in the North. "Exceptional men," he said, the "talented tenth," should lead the masses of blacks. They should insist on their full rights, "including the right to vote."[33] In the summer of 1905, Du Bois and twenty-nine other black intellectuals organized the Niagara Movement, dedicated to the struggle for black equality. Very little was heard from the organization until a full-scale race riot took place in 1908 in Lincoln's birthplace, Springfield, Illinois.[34]

Niagara Movement members immediately published a call for a new civil rights organization. A number of prominent white leaders answered the appeal, including several descendants of abolitionists, a number of prominent German Jewish leaders, and a few Russian Jews. On February 12, 1909, they announced the formation of the NAACP. Du Bois founded and edited the NAACP's influential monthly magazine, the *Crisis*. A year later, the interracial National Urban League formed to battle discrimination in housing and employment.[35]

Meanwhile, economic necessity rather than opposition to Booker T. Washington's ideas impelled many black southerners to leave home. An insidious insect, the boll weevil, had spread throughout the South, and was chewing away at the cotton crop. Floods also destroyed many fields. It became impossible to earn even the barest living from the land.

At first, many rural black farmers sought factory work in southern cities. Excluded from decent jobs, from 1915 on through the 1920s, a million and a half African Americans headed north in a so-called Great Migration. As factories started churning out materiel for the World War I Allies—England, France, and Russia—and as immigration from Europe came to a near standstill, labor recruiters headed south. Some even offered free transportation to workers. Black newspapers in northern cities encouraged southern blacks to leave the land of lynching and head for a better life. "To die from the bite of frost is far more glorious than at the hands of a mob," the *Chicago Defender* editorialized. Robert Abbott, founder of the newspaper, called for an exodus out of the South, like "the flight out of Egypt."[36] Chicago, Detroit, New York, and smaller midwestern and eastern cities saw their black populations double and triple.

Life in the northern cities was no picnic for African Americans. Housing and job discrimination were rigidly in place, although most new arrivals were able to find at least unskilled jobs. Furthermore, in the North they were allowed to vote.[37] They could also protest discrimination and even join the NAACP or the Urban League, without necessarily facing a beating or a lynch mob.

But just as the established German Jewish leaders had looked askance at the flood of Eastern European immigrants, the "talented tenth" worried that the behavior of the southern blacks would reflect poorly on them. The National Urban League set about "civilizing" and "Americanizing" the migrant. The *Chicago Defender*, no longer so enthusiastic about the exodus from Egypt, editorialized about "the habits of life little better than hottentots." A leading African American historian, Carter G. Woodson, predicted that "the maltreatment of the Negroes will be nationalized by this exodus. The poor whites of both sections will strike at this race."[38]

In 1915, the NAACP organized its first major public protest. Targeted was the new smash hit silent film *Birth of a Nation*, produced and directed by D. W. Griffith, a wealthy Christian from Louisville, Kentucky. Griffith's film portrayed Ku Klux Klansmen as heroes and black Reconstruction politicians as corrupt cowards. Worse yet, an evil-looking black man was shown chasing a virginal white woman, who jumped off a cliff to avoid his advances. Earlier silent films made by another Christian, Thomas Edison, with titles like *Watermelon Contest* and *King Cotton*, had been bad enough, portraying black Americans as either fools or happy slaves. Edison and Griffith had also managed to produce a few less than flattering films about Jews.[39] But no earlier film had received the promotional ballyhoo of *Birth of a Nation*. Long picket lines marched in front of theaters urging the public to boycott Griffith's film. The pickets did not have much success, but the NAACP gained a reputation as the leader in the struggle of African Americans.[40]

Racial conflict escalated in northern cities as poor blacks competed with poor whites, many of whom were also from the South, for scarce, substandard housing and unskilled jobs, just as Woodson had predicted. Bloody riots broke out, the most violent of them in East St. Louis. On July 28, 1917, fifteen thousand blacks silently paraded in New York City to condemn the rising tide of white racism.

Soon, African American participation in the U.S. armed

forces became the central focus of the NAACP's attention as the United States prepared to enter World War I.[41] The U.S. Army was completely segregated, as was the Navy, and the Marine Corps completely barred black enlistees.

A riot in Houston involving African American troops concluded with the execution of several black soldiers and was used as a rationale to limit black participation in the war effort and as an argument against integrating the army.

Du Bois, believing that patriotism would eventually pay off for black Americans, wrote an editorial in the *Crisis* urging black men to volunteer to fight, forget their "special grievances," and "close ranks" with whites in the fight for democracy.[42] Many blacks went along with Du Bois's advice, hoping that the slogan "Save the World For Democracy" would include them. The opposite happened. Contingents of black soldiers were led by white southern officers who openly insulted them. Stationed in the South, they were tormented by townspeople and barred from restaurants and other public places. Of 350,000 drafted blacks, only 40,000 were allowed to see combat, most of them assigned to fight in the allied French army. The American command advised the French officers to keep their men from socializing with the black troops, telling them that blacks were dangerous. The French for the most part ignored the advice and awarded France's highest honor, the Croix de Guerre, to three of the four black divisions that had been attached to French army units.

Jews also faced heightened discrimination. Russian Jews were suspicious of a wartime alliance that included czarist Russia, home of the pogroms. Jews became a special government target of persecution when the United States joined the Allies on April 6, 1917. Other Americans were also confused by the war. Some Irish immigrants supporting freedom for Ireland wanted no part of a war that included Great Britain as an ally. Germans felt sympathy for the country of their birth, the new enemy. The Socialist Party, by then the nation's third largest, was rent with disputes over participation in the war. Black, Jewish, and many other ethnic group leaders were also divided.[43]

One way to achieve a wartime spirit was to frighten those

who spoke out against joining the conflict. Accordingly, the Espionage Act of 1917 and the Sedition Act of 1918 were passed to silence the opposition. In New York City, Morris Hillquit, one of the signers of the Socialist Party's antiwar St. Louis Platform, ran for mayor after war had been declared. He was defeated as the majority of American Jews went along with their government decision, joined the army, and sang patriotic songs along with everyone else. Although there were incidents of social discrimination in the armed forces, there was little or no official anti-Semitism. Jews made up a little over 3.27 percent of the total population but almost 6 percent of the armed forces. More than nine thousand of them served as commissioned officers, including one general. Over a thousand medals were awarded to Jewish fighters, including three Congressional Medals of Honor.[44]

Nevertheless, all Jews were attacked for the antiwar sentiments of a small minority. Police attended political meetings on the Lower East Side, especially those conducted in Yiddish. Deportation proceedings were begun against several union and radical leaders who were not yet citizens. Immigrants lived in fear.

After the war, Jewish veterans marched in ticker-tape parades along with other white returning veterans. But black soldiers, many of them still in uniform, were greeted by violence in the North and in the South. White racists could not stand the sight of an African American proudly wearing a military uniform.

The worst incident took place in Chicago during the last week of July 1919.[45] Three days of violence started at a beach on July 27 when a seventeen-year-old black boy swam across an invisible segregation line and was stoned and drowned by a group of white boys. When black adults asked the police to arrest the culprits, they refused. Gangs of whites swept into black neighborhoods. Twenty black people and fourteen white people died, and 537 were injured in the next five days; many black homes were burned down.

Race riots spread through two dozen cities and towns during what would be called the Red Summer of 1919. A disappointed W. E. B. Du Bois changed his advice: "we are cowards and jackasses if now that the war is over we do not marshal every ounce of our brain and brawn to fight a sterner, longer, more unbending battle against the forces of hell in our land," he declared.[46]

African Americans had very few allies in their "unbending battle." Weakened by internal conflict over support for World War I, the Socialist Party could do little more than write about the problems of African Americans. In 1917, another event just about destroyed it. A revolution replaced Russian czardom with a Communist government. Revolutionary leader Vladimir Lenin, promising to bring prosperity to the workers, made a separate peace with Germany. Many socialists believed that the new Soviet government would bring hope to all humanity. They blamed the capitalist system for all of the miseries of workers and for racism and anti-Semitism. As the United States and its Allies sent troops to Russia in a vain attempt to crush Lenin's new Soviet regime, the Socialist Party split over the so-called Russian question. Most of the departing members eventually regrouped to help found the American Communist Party.[47]

When World War I ended in 1919, war-supply plants fired excess employees and over four million workers went on strike. To counter the rising tide of postwar labor organizing, the Federal Bureau of Investigation (FBI) was established under the leadership of J. Edgar Hoover. A full-scale "Red Scare" was launched by Attorney General A. Mitchell Palmer. In January 1920, government agents broke into homes and meeting halls, without search warrants, and arrested unionists, socialists, anyone whose name appeared on the list Hoover had compiled for the Palmer raids. Meetings conducted in Yiddish were especially suspect. Up to ten thousand people were arrested and denied legal representation; hundreds were deported. Caught up in the atmosphere of fear, the New York State Legislature refused to seat five elected Socialist members. In 1917, seventeen teachers were charged with disloyalty at De Witt Clinton High School. Eleven of them were Jewish. Three of the Jewish teachers were fired.[48] When the Red Scare ended, the job had been done. The Socialist Party existed only as a ghost of its former self; most reformers had been silenced.[49]

In 1920, Henry Ford launched a full-scale war against "Jew

Bolsheviks" in the pages of his newspaper, the *Dearborn Independent*, with a readership of over 600,000. He published a fraudulent document, known as the Protocols of the Elders of Zion, which was supposedly a Jewish master plan to take over the world. Later, Adolf Hitler would use this same tract as a rationale for the Nazi Holocaust. A fear of unions seemed to underlie Ford's frontal assault on Jews. Ford had commented to an interviewer that Jews had organized unions "to interrupt work." Under a barrage of unified Jewish protest, in 1927 Ford publicly apologized for his one-man war against the Jews, and many believed he had seen the error of his ways. Actually, a boycott of his automobiles, as well as a threatened lawsuit, had caused his sudden conversion to tolerance.[50]

While Ford's campaign was at its height, many colleges had set up usually secret quota systems to screen out Jewish applicants. In New York, Columbia University and New York University sharply cut the number of Jewish students entering after World War I. Jewish students turned to the free colleges in New York City—City College and Hunter College. In 1922 Harvard's president, Abbott Lawrence Lowell, announced that a new admissions policy to limit the number of Jewish students was under discussion.

> *Today Jews are practically ostracized from social organizations ... if there were fewer Jews, this problem would not be so.*[51]

His words bore a startling resemblance to the rationales for the May Laws passed in czarist Russia in 1882, supposedly to "shield the Russian population against harmful Jewish activity."

In that atmosphere, the immigration restrictionists won their thirty-five year crusade.[52] Congress passed the Immigration Laws of 1924, which set up a national-origins quota system for immigrants, giving northwestern Europe the largest quotas. It was commonly believed that President Calvin Coolidge had "signed an immigration law to restrict the entrance of Jews from eastern Europe."[53] Three years earlier, in an article in *Good Housekeeping*, Coolidge had bluntly stated that "biological laws show us that Nordics deteriorated when mixed with other races."[54]

These troubles were soon forgotten by most Americans as industrialization moved rapidly forward. For the first time consumerism became a major passion as people rushed to buy automobiles, furniture, and electrical appliances. The installment plan allowed a growing middle class to indebt itself in order to purchase the new products. Industrial output nearly doubled, profits skyrocketed, and wages increased. For millions, however, from black sharecroppers in the South to low-paid black workers in the North and white factory workers scraping by, the Roaring Twenties did not represent a dream come true.

By then a new unity had emerged among Americanized second-generation Jews concerned about anti-Semitism. On the one hand, Jews were labeled wild-eyed subversives; on the other hand, they were called wealthy, greedy bankers. The reality was that the daughters and sons of garment workers trying to find employment as office workers found it almost impossible to land a job.[55] Many firms officially excluded Jews.[56] Want ads and real estate listings openly stated: "No Jews need apply."

Young Jewish professionals—engineers, doctors, and lawyers—either had to find work outside of their professions or face discrimination. For graduating Jewish medical students, it was almost impossible to find the required internships. Massachusetts General Hospital appointed its first woman intern in 1919. The administrators duly recorded that their choice had been restricted to the lady doctor or one of two "undesirable male Hebrews."[57] Even the few Jews who became professionals and could afford to pay higher rents were barred from apartments in some neighborhoods of Manhattan and Queens. In Los Angeles, public schools offered occupational training for minorities after making "surveys of the occupations suitable to firms employing Negro, Mexican, and Jewish help."[58]

No official anti-Semitic laws existed, but occasional acts of violence did occur. In the summer of 1927 *The New York Times* reported that at Kings County Hospital in Brooklyn three Jewish interns were assaulted, gagged, bound, and showered with ice water by a couple of dozen coworkers.[59]

Many children of immigrant Irish, Italians, Scandinavians, and Slovaks had learned their fathers' trades and won union apprenticeships. Anti-Semitism in the trades and restrictions in the professions caused most second-generation Jewish youth to look for more open avenues to earning a living. Many entered the rapidly growing public school system as low-paid teachers. A handful of others struck it rich through sheer luck.

Jewish immigrants like Carl Laemmle, Adolf Zukor, Louis B. Mayer, and Benjamin Warner worked as peddlers and at other low-paying jobs. Investing a few hundred dollars in what was then considered a risky, marginal business, they rented and showed silent films in tiny storefront rooms.[60]

Vaudeville shows cost a quarter in those days, and theater seats went for half a dollar—too much for many laborers. But thousands of workers could afford to pay the five-cent admission to the Nickelodeons where they would watch in amazement as a moving train roared silently toward a woman tied to the tracks, or a posse hunted down a criminal. By 1908 over a hundred nickelodeons were operating in New York City alone, many of them on the Lower East Side.

It was anti-Semitism that eventually pushed the nickelodeon owners into film production. Thomas Edison, embroiled in court cases to prove that he was the inventor of the motion picture projector, ran one of the largest silent film production companies and attempted to form a monopoly with other Protestants to drive out the Jewish distributors. Several of the Jewish distributors went out to California and founded their own production companies—Columbia Pictures, Paramount, Fox, and Warner Brothers. They knew the tastes of the predominantly ethnic young audiences, and soon they were on their way to success.

Pushing the Americanization theme, they included very few African Americans in their early silent films. A few "Hollywood Jews" like Jack Goldberg financed black-owned production companies like the Colored Players and the Lincoln

Production Company, which made all-black "race movies." Blacks built up their own Hollywood in the Watts area of Los Angeles. They "boasted of such victories as entering a black float in the Rose Bowl parade . . . spent holidays in Santa Monica and complained bitterly when doors were closed against them."[61] With less backing and smaller audiences, the black film industry achieved only brief success, collapsing completely when "talking movies" arrived on the scene.

Most Jewish immigrants never found their way to fame and fortune in Hollywood or anyplace else. Some Jewish couples opened mom-and-pop groceries, clothing stores, and candy stores in their own neighborhoods, such as East Harlem. By 1930, Harlem was rapidly becoming a segregated African American slum as most Italians and Jews moved elsewhere. But Jewish shopkeepers often could not afford to relocate their businesses to higher-rent areas where they would have to build up new clientele from scratch. Other Jews held jobs in Harlem, sometimes as managers of apartment houses owned by prosperous Christian firms. Excluded from better opportunities by the widespread anti-Semitism of the day, Jewish shopkeepers found themselves the visible and sometimes hated "other" in black neighborhoods.

With mass actions almost impossible to organize in the prevalent atmosphere of conformity, fear, and thought control, leaders of African American and Jewish organizations turned to less public activities. A significant group of Jewish Americans worked for the establishment of a Jewish state in Palestine through groups such as the World Zionist Organization. Few wanted to settle in a Jewish state, but they celebrated when a joint resolution of Congress in 1922 approved "the establishment in Palestine of a national home for the Jewish people."[62]

The NAACP concentrated on court cases pertaining to civil rights. W. E. B. Du Bois attempted to fulfill his dream of establishing a thriving black culture. He helped launch the Harlem Renaissance, a celebration by the "talented tenth" of their many literary and artistic abilities. New York became a center for African American writers, musicians, and artists. Wealthy African Americans and whites came to Harlem to attend art exhibits and to listen to black jazz artists, comics, and singers in nightspots like the famous Cotton Club. Many black writers and artists depicted the hard lives of African Americans, but most poor black people never read their books or saw their paintings.

A new leader emerged and captured the allegiance of millions of African Americans. In 1914 a Jamaican named Marcus Garvey founded the Universal Negro Improvement Association in his own country. In 1917, he relocated to New York City and started a branch there.

Garvey's message was simple: America would never give blacks equality because racism was too deeply embedded in the culture; blacks would have to set up their own businesses, become black capitalists, help themselves, and prepare to resettle in Africa. By the mid-1920s, Garvey's movement had spread to thirty-eight states and become the largest black mass movement in American history. After an initial interest in Zionism, however, Garvey became increasingly anti-Jewish.

Du Bois was briefly interested in Garvey's brand of black nationalism, but Garvey did not return the favor. Garvey considered capitalism of great benefit to world progress and considered socialists "enemies of human advancement." Du Bois had long been interested in socialist ideas and considered the struggle for political rights primary.

The pennies and nickels of poor black people were simply inadequate to compete with powerful white businesses and bring Garvey's black capitalist dream to fruition. Shipbuilders sold him leaky vessels for the trips to Africa, and he was persecuted by federal agencies. Convicted of mail fraud, Garvey served two years in Atlanta Prison and then was deported. He died in London in 1940, the poor and forgotten "father of black nationalism."

In the mid-1920s, perhaps because of the brief but astonishing success of the Garvey movement and the failure of the Harlem Renaissance to produce a black cultural identity, Du Bois joined forces with A. Philip Randolph, a black union organizer. Randolph, the son of a poor Florida preacher, had moved to Harlem in 1911 and converted to socialism. Unlike Du Bois,

Marcus Garvey (center), a Jamaican leader who advocated black nationalism and self-reliance, was deported by the U.S. government. Garvey was also anti-Zionist.

he had opposed America's entry into World War I and had become the target of Attorney General Palmer, who called him "the most dangerous black in America."[63] Although he supported the Harlem Renaissance, Randolph, who was more concerned with the problems of black workers than with the careers of the "talented tenth," organized the Brotherhood of Sleeping Car Porters in 1925. He believed that the socialists were the only white people in America who cared about African Americans.

As the Great Migration brought them north, southern black workers had found their most consistent allies in the ranks of the Jewish poor. There was unconditional Jewish support for black victims of racism. "No organ of Jewish public opinion failed to express some degree of sympathy and commiseration with the plight of black people," historian Hasia Diner concluded.[64]

Even the most conservative anti–labor union Yiddish newspaper, the *Yiddishe Tageblatt* (Jewish Daily News), representing the Orthodox communities, ran articles against antiblack racism. But the most influential publication, Abraham Cahan's socialist *Jewish Daily Forward*, paid special attention to the problems of African Americans. Regular articles condemned lynching and published reports of black poverty, legal and civil rights victories, and the outstanding record of blacks in uniform. The *Forward* also ran statements by black leaders like Du Bois and Randolph.

The Yiddish newspapers did not hesitate to support black self-defense against what they often called "pogroms," cheering any sign of black aggressiveness while most American newspapers cringed at the thought. In its coverage of the East St. Louis riot of July 1917, the *Forward* described white racists as "bloodthirsty . . . wild beasts" as they "set on fire the Negro quarter." Even the more conservative *Tageblatt* reported that: "The ground in East Saint Louis drank human blood, shed by citizens of the most civilized country in the world."[65]

The German Jewish community published dozens of journals and one English-language daily newspaper. These periodicals often featured articles stressing Americanization and the

Striking members of the International Ladies' Garment Workers' Union (ILGWU) sit down in 1937 in Kansas City, Missouri, to prevent anyone from entering the plant.

success stories of prominent Jewish men. After the Frank lynching, however, they also carried articles on racism and lynching in the South, and they supported legislation outlawing lynching. During the Harlem Renaissance, they ran reviews in their entertainment pages praising the performances of black singers and actors.

But newspaper and magazine articles did not put bread on the tables of African American families. Few of the gains made by labor had an effect on black workers, who were kept out of most unions. The Socialist-led ILGWU, a rare exception to these racist policies, made real efforts to include African Americans in its organizing drives. Many black women earned their living as seamstresses and tailors, most of them working at home. Only a few black women participated in the garment strikes of 1909–10, but as the war and immigration legislation cut off the flow of working-class immigrants from Europe, the number of black garment workers in the factories slowly climbed.

In the 1920s, Rose Schneiderman made sure that union meetings were conducted in English rather than Yiddish so that African American women could participate. The Urban League in 1923 praised the interracial garment shops in Chicago. The New York chapter of the ILGWU held organizing meetings for black garment workers. A. Philip Randolph, a stirring speaker, helped attract crowds, and the union hired black organizers.

Most Americans were not readers of the Yiddish press and knew or cared little about the problems of minorities as they struggled to be part of the emerging society of fun and consumerism. Many U.S.-born Jews had the same attitudes held by their Protestant and Catholic counterparts. African Americans, along with Mexican Americans and Native Americans, remained for the most part in the backwaters of the Roaring Twenties, most of them losing hope of sharing in the much heralded economic boom.

Behind the scenes, trouble was brewing in the economy. The boom was about to go bust.

Chapter

FOUL-WEATHER FRIENDS

In 1929, another reason for banning new arrivals emerged—
the Great Depression.[1] Cycles of prosperity had always been
followed by economic downturns, but this crisis lasted longer
and affected more people. Americans knew that each day could
bring news that their jobs were gone. A knock at their door
could mean that the city marshal had arrived, ready to dump
their furniture and clothing out on the street because they had
not paid their rent. Millions of unemployed men and women
roamed the nation, searching for work of any kind. When those
who had managed to set aside savings for a rainy day went to
withdraw their money, they found locked doors at permanently
closed banks.

At first people were too shocked to do much, but soon
unprecedented alliances formed between odd partners like
black sharecroppers and white tenant farmers in the South and
Jews and African Americans in city slums. A powerful new
union movement, the Congress of Industrial Organizations
(CIO), was born after many bloody struggles.

Radicals, socialists, Communists, and anarchists had long
preached that the capitalist system benefited only the rich. Few
had listened to them in the 1920s, when even many of the
poor were convinced that they could win a small piece of the
American dream. But as the dark clouds of the Depression
refused to budge, the arguments of the Left seemed to make
some sense.

On March 6, 1930, about a million people took part in
"hunger marches" all over the country, breaking into food ware-

houses and taking what they needed. These incidents were only an early indication of the desperate rage that many Americans felt. Oklahoma attorney Oscar Ameringer informed Congress: "The masses . . . say that this government is a conspiracy against the common people."[2]

African Americans felt the sting of the Depression more sharply than any other group.[3] The conservative New York *Herald Tribune* reported that "Rising resentment against the existing social system is the outstanding motif of Harlem at the present time."[4] There was no welfare system in those days. President Herbert Hoover believed that people should pull themselves up by their own bootstraps. Harlem's churches served thousands of free meals a week.

As the hopes of the 1920s turned to dust in every corner of the nation, radicals formed the Trade Union Unity League (TUUL) and the Unemployed Councils. Many of the organizers were Jewish Americans, often the grown children of socialist garment workers. One of the earliest tests of the unemployed councils and TUUL took place in Detroit in early 1932. America's chief anti-Semite of the 1920s, Henry Ford, had banned the hiring of Jews, fearing they would organize unions. Ford did hire African Americans, but he segregated them in his "black department," where they were trapped in dead-end unskilled jobs. Most of them lived in a segregated neighborhood called "Inkster."[5] By August 1931, as fewer cars were sold, paychecks were cut. By the end of the year, the Detroit plant had closed.

Ford had long used a team of secret police to spy on his workers and fire any who tried to unionize the plant. Since auto workers were out of work anyway, it didn't matter much to them whether their leaders were Communists, Socialists, Democrats, or Republicans. Any action seemed better than starving to death. On March 7, 1932, TUUL and Detroit Unemployed Council members led a hunger march of thousands of unarmed workers to the employment offices of the Ford Motor Company's River Rouge plant in Dearborn, Michigan. In the bitter cold, they were huddled together listening to speeches when bullets suddenly rained down on them from submachine guns located on an overpass and behind the factory gate. Four marchers fell dead and sixty were wounded.

The massacre only increased support for the movement. Five days later, six thousand workers marched down Detroit's main thoroughfare, Woodward Avenue. From all over the nation came letters of support and contributions to the Unemployed Council of Detroit.[6]

In Moscow, Soviet leaders advised American Communist Party leaders to make fresh efforts to build a unified black and white organization. U.S. Communists were instructed to convince African Americans that they should regard all other groups claiming to represent them—the NAACP, black nationalists, militant church leaders, Socialist Party leaders such as A. Philip Randolph—and all others who disliked the Soviet brand of socialism—as political opponents.

Harlem, the largest black ghetto in the nation, became the major focus of Communist activity. The Soviet Comintern invited a few black Communists on all-expense-paid trips to Moscow. They came back to Harlem claiming that racism no longer existed under socialism and that the Soviet Union had escaped the Depression, which had quickly spread all over Europe.

But very few of Harlem's African Americans were interested in discussions about the merits of capitalism versus socialism. Their response to talk of black-white labor unions was skeptical. Among those lucky enough to have work at all, almost half held isolated unskilled jobs as maids, porters, janitors, or laundry workers, and union talk had a way of getting one fired quickly. Furthermore, most of the unions had refused to enroll black members in the past.

Half of Harlem's black residents had been born in the South, and the interracial membership of the Communist Party undoubtedly worried them. They had learned at their parents' knees that mixing between the races could mean death. When troubles hit, they went for help to their families, friends, and churches. Religious organizations recruited thousands of new members. The Father Divine movement taught pride and self-respect and offered cheap meals to the Father's "angels." Communists had nothing good to say about religion, labeling it "the opiate of the masses."

With direct recruiting to the Harlem Communist Party branch a dismal failure, and jobs the main thing on everyone's mind, activists put their energy into the Unemployed Councils. Teams of energetic young white people, many of them Jewish, descended on Harlem.[7] Some lived in East Harlem, which was still home to about 15,000 Jews in the early Depression years. Others were students at nearby City College, and a handful trickled in from the wealthier halls of ivy of Columbia University.

Harlem Unemployed Council members mounted impressively large protest rallies at City Hall, demanding relief payments for starving families. The New York State Legislature agreed to appropriate $20 million for relief and open local offices to distribute the funds. When many of the hungry waited as long as four months before they got so much as a dollar, Unemployed Council members sat in at the relief centers and were sometimes beaten by police who were called in to disperse them. The word spread through Harlem that whites were willing to get beaten up along with blacks.

By 1933, almost a fifth of the nation's 12 million blacks were receiving tiny checks that barely warded off starvation— twice the number of white recipients. Two years later, unemployed blacks outnumbered whites three to one.[8]

In the wake of the victory for home relief, dozens of new organizations sprang up overnight and old ones revived. One of them, the International Labor Defense (ILD), founded in 1925 as an interracial legal action group for immigrants, unionists, and blacks,[9] started focusing on black prisoners in 1930 and named a black Communist, attorney William L. Patterson, as its national secretary. The ILD sponsored dozens of meetings on the streets of Harlem, protesting lynching and police brutality.

Other groups swung into action. The People's Committee against Discrimination in Harlem Hospital demanded decent health care. When families were evicted from their apartments, interracial defense squads showed up and moved the furniture back inside while onlookers clapped and cheered. Langston Hughes, Harlem's unofficial poet laureate from the Harlem Renaissance days, led the newly created League of Struggle for Negro Rights (LSNR). Black children were offered free vacations in upstate summer camps where they mixed with the children of white (mostly Jewish) radicals, sang union songs and learned Russian folk dances.

The openly interracial composition of these groups was something new for Harlemites. It was common knowledge that the NAACP and the Urban League had many behind-the-scenes white supporters aiding and financing their work, but it was not an ordinary sight to see black men and women working together with whites and even occasionally holding hands in public. Word also spread quickly that white Communists were sharply reprimanded if they behaved disrespectfully toward African Americans. Interracial social events became common. At one much-talked-about dance, Duke Ellington's band played for an integrated crowd.[10]

In 1931, in the small Alabama town of Scottsboro, the arrest of nine young African American men, ages thirteen to twenty-one, led to the first nationwide alliance between African Americans and white Americans, many of them Jewish. The nine were arrested and charged with assault and battery for a scuffle with white unemployed men on a freight train. Two young white women, Ruby Bates and Victoria Price, were also found on the train. Within a few hours, the assault charges were converted into charges of black gang rape. All of the evidence appeared to contradict the charges, but this was Alabama, and just being black was sufficient evidence of wrongdoing for most. Angry crowds gathered near the jail, screaming for blood.

Within two weeks, all but the youngest defendant, a thirteen-year-old, were tried, convicted, and sentenced to death. Lawyers quickly filed an appeal on behalf of "the Scottsboro Boys," who soon became the foremost symbol of the struggle against racist oppression in the 1930s.[11]

At first the NAACP was reluctant to become involved in a

rape case, but the ILD had no such reservations. It approached all of Harlem's groups and leaders, from the Urban League to the Reverend Adam Clayton Powell, Jr., then assistant pastor at his father's Abyssinian Baptist Church, persuading them to join together in the Scottsboro Defense Committee. The Communist Party retained a leading constitutional lawyer, who won a stay of execution from the U.S. Supreme Court, which agreed to review the Alabama trial later in 1932.

The NAACP finally examined the trial records and decided the boys were innocent. It then tried to take over control from the International Labor Defense. The Scottsboro nine and their parents were caught squarely in the middle. The NAACP believed that ILD tactics such as large public demonstrations would destroy any chance for a new and fair trial. The ILD responded that it was impossible for blacks to receive a fair trial in Alabama and that only united pressure from blacks and whites could save the nine. The Scottsboro boys' parents chose to stick with the ILD.

Mass meetings and marches of thousands of people took place throughout the nation. African American and Jewish newspapers gave almost daily coverage to the Scottsboro cause.[12] The National Committee for the Defense of Political Prisoners was formed by members of the "talented tenth." It raised thousands of dollars at a mammoth dance featuring both white and black entertainers. Harlem's *Amsterdam News*, which had originally supported the NAACP, now urged its readers to join the ILD's defense committees. On November 7 the U.S. Supreme Court ordered a new trial.

Meanwhile, as the Scottsboro Boys languished in their cells, German democracy crumbled before the advance of Adolf Hitler and his Nazi movement. Fearful of Germany's rising strength and Hitler's frequent talk of "a new order" and a German Europe, the Soviet government began to think in terms of unity against fascism rather than an all-out war against liberals and anti-Soviet socialists such as A. Philip Randolph. Moscow instructed Communist parties all over the world to join with former rivals in alliances or parliamentary governments termed a "United Front" against fascism.

Then a break came in the Scottsboro case when, at the sec-

Seven "Scottsboro Boys" with their attorney,
Samuel Liebowitz (second from left), in 1932
at the Jefferson, Alabama, jail

ond trial, Ruby Bates, one of the alleged victims, admitted that
the police had forced her to lie. Despite a brilliant defense by
prominent Jewish defense attorney Samuel Liebowitz, a leading member of the Democratic Party, the prosecutors advised
the jury to prove "that Alabama justice cannot be bought and
sold with Jew money from New York." Two hundred men met
that night and talked about "riding the New York lawyers out
of town on a rail and then lynching the Scottsboro Boys."[13]

When the expected guilty verdict was handed down, hundreds marched to New York's Pennsylvania Station to greet Liebowitz and then parade up Broadway to Harlem. Most of Harlem endorsed the ILD and pressured the NAACP to end its hostilities.[14] Alabama justice, they said, had been exposed.

Pressured from all quarters, the NAACP finally offered its aid, and a united front defense entered full bloom. As mass protests grew even larger, in late June 1933, Judge James Horton, who had presided at the second trial, overturned the jury's verdict and called for a third trial. By then the International Labor Defense had opened nine new chapters in Harlem, each named after a Scottsboro defendant. But in the fall of 1934, two ILD attorneys were arrested for trying to bribe Ruby Bates's companion, Victoria Price. A furious Liebowitz joined the NAACP in calling for the removal of the ILD from the case. While the nine young men remained in jail for a third year, the NAACP reached a fragile agreement with the ILD, and a broader Scottsboro Defense Committee was formed. This time the NAACP won its demand for a curtailment of mass protests and a greater concentration on legal efforts.

The last trial in 1936 ended once again in a guilty verdict. After five years in jail, the desperate young men and their parents agreed behind the scenes to a plea bargain in 1937. Four of the defendants were released, four more served long sentences and then were pardoned, and the ninth escaped from jail and was never recaptured. But the lives of the Scottsboro Boys had been saved, and the united-front alliance spilled over into dozens of movements, peopled largely by blacks and Jews, to improve Harlem's schools, hospitals, and relief agencies and to force local merchants to hire black workers.

At this time, only a few Americans, most of them Jewish, noticed the beginnings of a terrible tragedy for European Jews, although a surprising number of African Americans also sounded an early alarm.[15] A black-owned newspaper, the *Washington Tribune*, reprinted statements from British newspapers warning that there would be a massacre of German Jews. The prestigious newspaper the *Afro-American* commented in an editorial on February 22, 1936: "Our Constitution keeps the

South from passing many of the laws Hitler has invoked against the Jews, but by indirection, by force and terrorism, the South and Nazi Germany are mental brothers."[16]

Hitler's new Nazi government passed a civil service law that excluded 600,000 German Jews, about 1 percent of the population of 60 million, from all public service jobs. Jewish teachers, as well as liberal non-Jews, were discharged. These events were not well publicized in mainstream U.S. newspapers, but a prestigious British newspaper, the *Manchester Guardian*, ran an article headlined "Nazi 'Purge' of the Universities, A Long List of Dismissals."[17]

Most of the scholars left Germany, many of them applying for scarce visas for entry to the United States. The Rockefeller Foundation set up an Emergency Rescue Committee in Aid of Displaced Foreign Scholars to find them teaching jobs. Most universities had maintained their Jewish quotas since the 1920s and made no job offers. Only a handful of usually smaller institutions hired one or two of the displaced scholars.[18]

The Emergency Rescue Committee wrote to hundreds of colleges, including a few in Latin America and South Africa. Not one of the hundred traditionally African American institutions was contacted until 1941, even though Howard University had written to the committee asking about the employment of displaced German scholars as early as 1934. Perhaps by word of mouth, however, one of the earliest appointments of a Jewish émigré scholar was made by Le Moyne-Owen, a small black institution in Memphis. On their own, twenty African American-run colleges eventually hired about fifty refugee Jewish professors who had been ignored by white institutions.

A few Jewish organizations urged Congress to ease immigration restrictions to allow persecuted Jews to enter the embrace of the Lady in the Harbor, but with joblessness still on the increase, the government was not interested in fresh arrivals, persecuted or not. Meanwhile, thousands of German Jews fled their homeland. At the German border, Nazi guards seized their money and any other valuables. Destitute, they arrived in European cities unemployed and hungry. In London, a committee was formed to raise funds for Jewish refugees.

Paul Robeson, a brilliant African American who had gained fame as a singer and actor during the heyday of the Harlem Renaissance, had decided to live in Europe to escape American racism and was starring in a play in London. He agreed to give a benefit performance to raise funds for the refugees, commenting, "The white people who have been kindest to me in America have been Jewish people."[19] Many black people agreed with him.

Many Jewish college graduates, barred by anti-Semitism from most private-sector jobs, worked as public school teachers, social workers in the slums, and librarians. In labor unions such as the Home Relief Employees Association, it was easy to win a fight for the hiring of blacks. But when the League of Struggle for Negro Rights (LSNR) learned that two of New York City's bus lines were planning to hire several hundred workers in early 1934, the task proved more difficult. League members in the Transport Workers Union (TWU) were only a handful among a distinctly antiblack group of mostly Irish workers who had long considered the bus lines their own private job world. When the LSNR launched a bus boycott against the Fifth Avenue Coach Company because of its policy of not hiring black drivers and mechanics, the Transport Workers Union refused its support. The lengthy boycott, joined by concerned whites, most of them Jewish, failed because for most working Harlemites the buses provided the only affordable means of transportation to their jobs. Nonetheless, the solidarity shown by the interracial pickets impressed people.

An ongoing united campaign against lynching was also put into high gear with the NAACP playing a leading role. Violence against blacks had increased alarmingly as angry unemployed southern whites took their hostility out on blacks. Antilynching legislation was regularly blocked in Congress by southern congressmen's filibusters.[20] Pressed to take action against the barbarism, President Franklin Delano Roosevelt publicly condemned lynching but refused to intervene. He was, after all, dependent on the support of southern legislators in the forthcoming 1936 election.

Harlem's African American residents were aware of a strong

*In 1934 NAACP members picket a
conference on crime to demand that
lynching be outlawed.*

Jewish presence among whites who fought against racism. During a police attack on an antilynching demonstration in 1934 outside of the Reverend Adam Clayton Powell's Abyssinian Baptist Church, for example, a young Jewish activist, Isadore Dorfman, had protected a young black woman. He was severely beaten for his trouble and remained close to death for several days. Just months later he showed up on a bus station picket line and was arrested. Dorfman became "something of a hero in the community."[21]

But far from Harlem, blaming the Jews became a national sport as hundreds of hate groups opened meeting halls and bookstores in many cities. Prominent Americans resurrected Henry Ford's old anti-Semitic campaign, lining up to support bigots like the Reverend Charles E. Coughlin, a Catholic priest. Despite Jewish Americans' distinguished record of combating anti-Catholicism,[22] Coughlin peddled his anti-Semitic hate poison in weekly radio broadcasts to about ten million listeners throughout the 1930s. Amazingly, Coughlin's supporters distributed his literature, filled with references to Nordic superiority, in black Detroit neighborhoods. Charles A. Lindbergh, America's aviation hero, fearing a second world war, joined Coughlin in blaming Jews for the Depression and in downplaying the Nazi threat.

But few if any African American leaders agreed with these hatemongers. Anti-Semitism in black neighborhoods was pretty much confined to street corners where some black nationalist agitators laced their speeches with virulent remarks about Jews. They seldom differentiated Jewish shopkeepers, pawnbrokers, landlords, rent collectors, and women who hired black servants at the Bronx "slave market"[23] from the radical Jewish students in the Unemployed Councils and the International Labor Defense.

Actually, most ghetto businesses and tenements, formerly owned by small investors including blacks and Jews, were lost during the Depression years to giant bank, real estate, and trust companies. Rent collectors were sometimes young jobless Jewish men, hired by the companies to take on the unpleasant job of dunning people for money. The invisible white landlord was the seldom seen "Mr. Charley," so hatred was focused on the rent collector, "Mr. Goldberg." Likewise, the powerful chain stores, like Grant's and Woolworth's, were owned by absentee millionaires. Italian, Jewish, and other white shopkeepers ran groceries, butcher shops, and other marginal businesses, often "hiring members of their own families" and living "behind and above the store."[24] They charged higher prices than the big chains, but sold on credit, cashed relief checks, and stayed open late.

Why did the nationalist African American street speakers focus on Jewish businessmen and not on the powerful industrialists and chain-store millionaires who blocked them from employment? Prominent African American Ralph Bunche later explained the reasons for anti-Semitism in black ghettos:

> *Negroes are an oppressed, frustrated people. Such a people hits always upon the simplest and most convenient explanation of its troubles. It pounces upon a scapegoat as a means of psychological escape. The Jew is handy.... And it is safe to scorn the Jew. His powers of retaliation are less great then those of the Gentile whites, for the Jew himself is a victim of race.*[25]

Dachau witness Paul Parks reflected the attitude of the majority of African Americans. The father of Parks's Jewish boyhood friend Gabriel Segal owned a grocery store in Indianapolis. During the Depression, Segal's father had sold Parks's mother groceries on credit and had given young Paul part-time work as well. Parks remembered that the Ku Klux Klan had tried to start a boycott of Jewish-owned businesses but failed. As far as he and his buddy Gabriel were concerned, the Klan and most white people considered them both "others." Parks went on to win a scholarship at Purdue University, where he was not permitted to live in the student dormitory. During his sophomore year he was welcomed at International House, which was open to foreign students, Jews, and blacks. Parks made friends with several Jewish students and concluded that of all the whites, Jews were the good guys.[26]

At the same time that black nationalists made anti-Semitic remarks on soapboxes, many African American parents, Garveyites included, trusted and appreciated Jewish teachers who worked in the ghetto schools. Throughout the early 1930s, a large number of radical teachers, "overwhelmingly Jewish,"[27] were assigned to Harlem. In college many of them had been told to get rid of their Jewish accents and even change their names. They became staunch fighters against racism in all of its ugly shapes. Together, Harlem teachers, both black and white, formed chapters of the Teachers Union and parent-teacher groups to fight for better conditions, nonracist textbooks, free lunches for hungry children, repairs in crumbling buildings, and new schools.

Alice Citron, a Jewish teacher, was not atypical. Her mother was a longtime member of the ILGWU, and at her home in East Harlem stories about her mother's union, rent strikes, and the struggle for social justice were common supper-table talk. Citron was an open Communist, but African American parents didn't seem to care. They only knew that when school authorities thought their children could barely learn, Alice Citron and other teachers like her had them performing plays, studying black history, and going on field trips to museums. Many employed African Americans also realized that unions with Jewish leadership and members, such as the Teachers Union, Musicians Union, Newspaper Guild, Relief Workers Association, and of course the ILGWU, were often the only ones willing to recruit black workers.[28]

A "Don't Buy Where You Can't Work" campaign in 1933, initiated by black nationalists and often targeting Jewish businessmen, is often cited as evidence of profound anti-Semitism in Harlem.[29] Actually, the final outcome of the nationalist boycott seems to prove the opposite. Several separate groups were campaigning around the issue. Sufi Abdul Hamid formed the Negro Industrial Clerical Alliance. Hamid has been called the first Black Muslim in Harlem. He preached on the virtues of Islam, sprinkling his harangues with a liberal dose of anti-Semitism. Later he marched around Harlem in boots and an imitation Nazi uniform, calling himself a "black Hitler."[30]

The Reverend John Johnson, a respected Harlem pastor, led another group that sent a delegation to Blumstein's department store, one of the few large Jewish-owned businesses in Harlem. The group turned over thousands of dollars in sales slips and demanded jobs. Several other church and community leaders, including Adam Clayton Powell, Jr., joined Johnson's group, forming an alliance, the Citizens League for Fair Play, in June 1934 to picket and boycott Blumstein's.

LSNR and Communist Party trade unionists, arguing unsuccessfully that the coalition should make sure that no white workers were fired when blacks were hired, joined the campaign. Over a three-month period, a number of stores, including Blumstein's, agreed to hire black clerks. When Sufi Abdul Hamid and other nationalists demanded that the new openings be given only to their followers, the coalition crumbled.

The Citizens League for Fair Play jumped into the vacuum and formed a new coalition to push for an end to discrimination in all jobs, trades, and professions. Its strategy was to gain the support of white union members for the hiring of black workers. It won a pivotal victory at the Empire Cafeteria, located in the heart of Harlem. Much of the cafeteria's lunch trade came from employees of a recently unionized relief office where many young radical Jewish social workers were employed. Less than two weeks after a boycott of the cafeteria was launched, honored by blacks and Jews alike, Empire hired four African American countermen without firing any white employees. The Empire victory impressed many moderate black leaders. The *Amsterdam News* and *New York Age* published condemnations of anti-Semitic street speakers.

The Yiddish and English-language Jewish newspapers seldom ran articles on anti-Semitism among blacks. Even when a black nationalist publication praised Nazi anti-Semitism, the *Forward* responded with an editorial about "the Jew who wakes up every day with the Scottsboro Boys on his mind."[31] The Jewish press gave full coverage to stories about blacks helping Jews, like a black minister in Newport News, Virginia, who prevented a mob from lynching a Jew. It published statements by groups of African Americans condemning anti-Semitism.

Jewish papers stated that any Jews who discriminated against blacks "should be stopped." The Jewish press pointed out the differences between the black nationalists behind Hamid and the majority of blacks, even generously stating that Sufi's followers had been "goaded on by the shattering effects of the Depression."[32]

Another important event that brought black nationalists into an interracial united front in 1934 was Italian dictator Benito Mussolini's decision to invade Ethiopia, an independent African nation next door to the Italian colony of Somalia. Black nationalists initially called for a boycott of Italian-owned stores and products and for a united black effort excluding whites. Black Communist leaders pointed out that more than 150,000 Italian Americans, most of them profoundly antifascist, lived in East Harlem, and that whites had played an important role in many movements to stop racism. In a clever move, they invited a prominent black nationalist to speak to an Italian Workers Club. When his speech was greeted by applause and a large sum of money was collected, the nationalists agreed to remain in an interracial coalition. A protest march was scheduled, and the proposed boycott of Italian merchants in Harlem was called off. On August 3, twenty-five thousand people paraded down Harlem's main thoroughfares. A huge contingent of Italians shouted "Hands off Ethiopia" in chorus with a black contingent, and then listened as a wide range of speakers compared fascists with lynch mobs.

In the 1934 elections, Democrats won an ovewhelming majority in Congress. The Works Progress Administration (WPA) created a work relief program that put millions of people to work building highways, bridges, public buildings, and dams. Their wages—an average $41.57 a month—provided little more than survival, but most people agreed that it was preferable to breadlines and even smaller home relief checks. It was hoped that the programs would also revive the economy by stimulating the production of steel and other needed materials.

Roosevelt appointed African Americans to several federal agencies. Mary McLeod Bethune was named director of Negro affairs for the National Youth Administration, and William H.

Hastie was named the first black federal judge. Much of Roosevelt's New Deal legislation came from old ideas, long advocated by immigrant Jewish socialists and liberals. The Social Security Act of 1935, for example, providing pensions for working people, had been proposed early in the century by two Jewish men, Isaac M. Rubinow and Abraham Epstein. They had won passage of an Old Age Security Act in New York State when Franklin Delano Roosevelt was governor. When Roosevelt was elected president in 1932, Epstein became a major lobbyist for national legislation.[33]

In the spring of 1935, New York garment union organizers launched a housewives' protest against high meat prices in Jewish neighborhoods. It expanded into Harlem, where black women from churches, nationalist groups, and radical organizations formed "flying squads" to picket butcher shops, demanding lower prices. After 4,500 butcher shops were forced to close down, meat prices were lowered.[34]

Throughout the rest of the year, rallies and demonstrations were an almost daily event in Harlem. Demands ranged from calls for a fair share of WPA jobs to increased relief payments, better housing, and even an end to Jim Crow in baseball and other sports. Banners fluttered in Harlem's breezes calling for rent strikes and spreading news of the latest lynchings in the South.

Conservatives tried to break the united front by blaming "Communist agitators" for a three-day riot that shook Harlem in March 1935. In response to the arrest of a young Puerto Rican boy caught shoplifting at the W. H. Kress store on 125th Street and rumors of his being beaten by police, crowds raced through Harlem's streets, smashing store windows and grabbing armfuls of food, clothing, and other goods. When the police managed to restore order, one rioter was dead and many had been injured or jailed.[35]

The police raided Communist Party headquarters and prosecutors blamed the "Reds" for the rioting. But the liberal mayor, Fiorello La Guardia, appointed six African American and five white Harlem citizens to a Mayor's Commission on Conditions in Harlem to hold public hearings on the riot's causes.

The hearings enhanced united-front efforts when most of

Harlem's organizations refused to make scapegoats of the local Communists, most of them Jews. They assembled all of the shocking facts on rampant discrimination in the nation's largest black ghetto—in home relief, education, and employment. In the wake of the publicity, a Harlem Committee for Better Schools was formed to launch a fight to "secure for the children of Harlem educational opportunities equal to the very best available to the most privileged child in New York City."[36] A year later the Harlem Committee had enough clout to force the transfer of a principal who had assaulted a fourteen-year-old black child and to win important curriculum changes and the promise of two new schools.[37]

By the mid-1930s, the new radical spirit had moved west to Hollywood. By then, filmmaking was a big business. Of eighty-five production companies in 1936, fifty-three of them were run by Jews, the original filmmaking pioneers and their offspring. Anti-Semites made Hollywood a favorite target, demanding that movies be taken "from hands of the devil of five hundred un-Christian Jews."[38] Caricatures of producers with exaggerated long noses and Star of David crowns appeared in right-wing publications. Most of the producers ignored the anti-Semitism frequently directed at them and created their own world, usually being careful to avoid Jewish subjects in their films.[39]

In the summer of 1934, Maurice Rapf, the teenage son of an MGM executive, returned from a visit to the Soviet Union filled with admiration for the new regime's anti-Nazi propaganda. His father asked Harry Warner to have a talk with his errant son.

"Don't forget you're a Jew," Warner scolded the boy. "Jewish Communists are going to bring down the wrath of the world on the rest of the Jews. Everybody thinks the Jews are Communists."

"I'll give up being a Communist if you give up being a capitalist," the youngster retorted. "Everybody thinks Jews are capitalists."

Producer David O. Selznick had different advice. "Be a radical," he said, "but don't wear it on your sleeve. . . . It's going to get in the way of your career."[40]

But a few of the Hollywood moguls could not forget that they were Jewish and had once had been poor. At Warner Brothers, one of the family sons, Harry, pushed to make films with a social message. During the 1930s, many young educated Jewish writers and actors from the East Coast were encouraged to come to work in Hollywood. Whatever their politics, many of the studio heads admired their talent. Leading an easy life on the West Coast, some of them could still not forget their socially conscious upbringing. They supported the antifascist Loyalists during the Spanish Civil War and started organizing unions. With the rise of Naziism, they stepped up their activities and formed the Hollywood Anti-Nazi League in 1936.

The Jewish producers were worried about Hitler too, especially when their film distribution offices in Germany were closed down in 1934 and the Los Angeles German-American Bund's radio attacks on Hollywood Jews escalated. The producers asked the Hollywood Anti-Nazi League to change its name to the Anti-Nazi Anti-Communist League, but they were turned down.

In January 1934, Representative Samuel Dickstein, an Eastern European-born Jew, unwittingly started an anti-Communist crusade that would color American democracy for the next twenty-five years. He introduced a Congressional resolution to create a committee that would investigate Nazi activities in the United States. Dickstein suggested that the new committee should be headed by a non-Jew so as to head off charges that Nazism was of interest only to Jews. Several hundred German Americans picketed the first sessions of the committee, shouting "Down with Dickstein" and "Heil, Hitler."

In 1937, Representative Martin Dies joined the investigation. Dies, who was the close friend of several well-known anti-Semites, rapidly transformed Dickstein's original committee into an anti-Communist, anti-Jewish investigatory group called the House Un-American Activities Committee (HUAC).

On the eve of negotiations between the Screenwriters Guild and the producers in 1939, Dies charged that the Hollywood Anti-Nazi League and the union were under the control of Communists. Dies's investigatory body, HUAC, told the producers to fire members of the Anti-Nazi League. The producers refused, telling the congressmen that the writers and actors were under contract. The committee returned to Washington and issued a report that would have an enormous impact in the future. It pinned the "un-American" label on anyone holding certain beliefs, including "absolute social and racial equality."[41]

In late 1935, Soviet leaders urged American Communists to form a "popular front of the working class with all other antifascist forces."[42] The survival struggles of African Americans were no longer to be a major focus of activity. Instead, friends made during the united-front effort would have to put their energy behind Roosevelt's reelection. The Communists believed that the Democrats were more likely than the Republicans to oppose fascism.

Behaving like a "left-wing extension of the Democratic Party,"[43] the Communists ran their own token candidate but threw their support behind Roosevelt. Staunch anti-Communist socialists like the *Forward*'s Abraham Cahan also believed that it was necessary to keep the New Deal administration in Washington. But they could not stomach the idea of voting for one of the capitalist parties, even as a lesser of evils. For Cahan, Roosevelt's party also represented crooked Tammany machine politicians in the North and racists in the South.

More than 85 percent of all Jewish Americans voted for Roosevelt in 1936. His administration had, after all, hired many Jewish college graduates, and it had passed the 1935 Wagner Act providing legal protection for millions of workers who wanted to hold elections to form unions.

Southern Democrats remained loyal to Roosevelt but for completely different reasons. The President had made important compromises to satisfy powerful southern agricultural interests (as well as growers in the West): farmworkers were not covered under the Wagner Act, and Roosevelt had made no move to protect the interracial Southern Tenant Farmworkers Union (STFU).

Two Jewish men, Howard Kester, a farmworkers' organizer, and Herman Goldberger, an attorney, were well aware of the terrible impact of Roosevelt's compromise with the southern Democrats, later known as "Dixiecrats." In the summer of 1934, men like Kester and Socialist Party leader Norman Thomas had helped Arkansas farmworkers form the STFU. For the first time sharecroppers, both black and white, and tenant farmers joined together in common cause. In early 1935, STFU leaders pressed the government for direct relief payments and an end to evictions and threats. In the offices of the federal Agricultural Adjustment Administration a behind-the-scenes fight took place when a handful of employees, a few young Jews among them, openly supported the sharecroppers and were fired. The emboldened growers decided to break the STFU completely. Many pickers were suddenly evicted from their homes, their meager possessions piled up on the road. Armed lawmen burst into a church in Earl, Arkansas, shot two people in the back, beat another into a coma, and fired on a crowd of fleeing churchgoers. Kester and Goldberger were pushed into a car and driven into the woods. One of the men who grabbed them was carrying a rope tied into a noose. Somehow Kester managed to talk the men out of a lynching. He and Goldberger were dumped near the Arkansas state line and told never to return.

At a campaign rally in Little Rock, Arkansas, on June 10, President Roosevelt refused to meet STFU leaders and publicly praised the leading representative of the growers.[44] Despite this outrage, Roosevelt gained a reputation as a friend of labor. Industrialists spent millions to defeat him and went to the courts to attempt to overturn the Wagner Act and prevent the newly formed CIO from holding elections in their mills and factories. Roosevelt made many bold pro-union speeches. In one he went so far as to say: "Concentration of economic power does not represent private enterprise as we Americans cherish it." It was his way of gathering the votes of America's workers and defeating socialist and communist ideology at the same time. He was promising to bring a kinder, gentler capitalism to America.

After Roosevelt's landslide 1936 victory, strikes swept over the industrial heartland. Even after the Supreme Court upheld the Wagner Act in 1937, dozens of corporations continued to refuse to allow union elections. At a Memorial Day rally in 1937, police responded to the call of Republic Steel officials and fired hundreds of shots into a crowd of picnicking unarmed workers and their families near the plant, killing nine people and wounding dozens more. Few Americans knew the truth about the tragic event. Most newspapers reported that the bloodshed had occurred at a Communist-inspired strikers' riot. Movie newsreels showing what had really happened did not reach the theaters.

CIO supporters around the nation demanded and finally won a congressional investigation. No amount of testimony could contradict what congressmen saw on the original newsreels. In the next months, elections were held throughout the steel industry. Unions were overwhelmingly supported at every steel mill.[45]

The right to unionize was a much celebrated victory that increased the popularity of the Roosevelt administration. Those engaged in the fight against fascism, however, grew more alarmed as the Nazi regime in Germany intensified its anti-Semitic campaign. In 1936, Spanish fascist general Francisco Franco launched a massive invasion of Spain from his post in Morocco with the intention of overthrowing the democratic Spanish Republic. Japan was busy overrunning China. Roosevelt, who had refused to act during the Italian invasion and conquest of Ethiopia, signed a Neutrality Act and refused to aid the Chinese or the Spanish Loyalists. Meanwhile, American businessmen were permitted to sell arms and oil to Italy, Germany, and Japan. Hitler and Mussolini in turn used the supplies to strengthen their own armies and to help Franco and the Japanese government.

Right after Christmas 1936, a contingent of American volunteers, calling themselves the Abraham Lincoln Brigade, among them many Jews and African Americans, sailed for Spain without government permission to join other young men from all over the world in International Brigades to help save Spanish democracy. They fought for three years, but without adequate arms and with the Germans testing their new air force over Spanish cities, Spain fell under fascist control in 1939. Many young Americans stayed behind, buried under Spanish soil.[46]

In the mid-1930s, most African Americans were more interested in black sports heroes like the famous boxer Joe Louis, "the Brown Bomber," and Olympic running star Jesse Owens, than in faraway struggles against fascism. Yet even the least politically aware black Americans were aware of the close link between their star athletes and the fight against Nazism and anti-Semitism.

Joe Louis, one of eight children in an Alabama sharecropper family, turned to professional boxing in 1934 after winning a Golden Gloves championship. When he won one fight after another, he should have been a logical contender for the heavyweight title but he was blocked by seemingly unbeatable racism in the sports world.[47] Louis's all-black management team turned to Mike Jacobs, a prominent Jewish sports promoter. Jacobs lined up an important fight between Louis and Italy's former heavyweight champion Primo Carnera, a favorite of facist dictator Benito Mussolini.

On June 25, 1935, as more than five hundred black volunteers signed up to fight the Italian fascists in Ethiopia, Louis knocked out Carnera. For many of the millions listening to radio broadcasts of the event, it was exactly as though the black Ethiopians had defeated the Italians. In the spring of 1936, Louis fought one of Adolf Hitler's heroes, German boxer Max Schmeling. Once again African Americans and Jews felt they had a stake in the fight. When Louis lost the bout, there were few dry eyes in black and anti-fascist Jewish neighborhoods. Louis would have to wait two years for a rematch.

Despite many protests, an American team participated in the 1936 Olympics in Berlin, Germany, Adolf Hitler's planned showcase for Aryan athletic prowess. Another black athlete, Jesse Owens, won three gold medals at the Berlin games—for the 100-meter dash, the 200-meter dash, and broad jumping, but the dictator refused to congratulate the black champion. In the relay event, the only two Jewish members of the American track team, Marty Glickman and Sam Stoller, were replaced to appease the Nazis, despite protests from Owens and the two replacements. Two months later Avery Brundage, president of the U.S. Olympics Committee, praised the Nazis at a pro-Hitler rally in Madison Square Garden.

Jesse Owens in his first win—the 100-meter dash—at the 1936 Olympic Games in Berlin, Germany. Jesse Owens won three gold medals at the Berlin Games, but Adolf Hitler refused to congratulate the black champion. The United States replaced two Jewish members of the track team to appease the Nazis.

Adolf Hitler speaking at a Nazi rally
at the Berlin Sports Palace

African Americans holding white-collar jobs in newly formed New Deal agencies took Adam Clayton Powell, Jr.'s advice to join interracial white-collar unions.[48] Nationalists continued to preach against interracialism, urging poor blacks to "think black, talk black, act black, and see black"[49] and peppering their street speeches with invective against Jews and Italians. But with the impact of CIO efforts to recruit black workers, and many young Jewish teachers and relief workers willing to help poor African Americans, anti-Semitism, rampant elsewhere in the nation, was at a low point in black ghettos.

Events in Europe continued to influence the political work of most antiracists. Ethiopia had fallen under Italian control, but the bloody conflict in Spain continued. In the spring of 1937, two African Americans who had died fighting in Spain were honored in leading Harlem churches. Black musicians Fats Waller and Count Basie played at a Carnegie Hall Concert for Spain sponsored by a Harlem and Musicians Committee for Spanish Democracy. One black leader later recalled that "Spanish freedom and Negro freedom were made to be synonymous."[50] The popular-front American League against War and Fascism was supported by almost every organization in black communities, from the Communists, the NAACP, and the Urban League to churches and even the Elks.

Most black leaders, although sharply critical of the Soviet regime, kept their silence during a disgraceful series of trials of dissidents in Moscow and a flood of rumors of slave labor camps in the "Socialist paradise." The Soviet Union, after all, was far from Harlem, and a number of prominent African Americans had returned from visits saying "you have more right to criticize in Russia than you could hope to have in Mississippi." Paul Robeson announced that he was sending his son to school in the Soviet Union in order to "escape race prejudice."[51]

African Americans needed all the help they could get, and Communists and their sympathizers were able to mobilize considerable white support for black causes. The *Amsterdam News* reflected the opinions of most black Americans when it admitted that the progress of the "Roosevelt Administration is the outcome of sustained agitation by Radicals and Liberals." The editors advised African Americans to "join those groups which are agitating for social and economic justice in the United States."[52]

A shadow was soon cast over these honeymoon days of this "Popular Front." Conservatives in Congress challenged the New Deal programs, and the Supreme Court declared several of them unconstitutional. Many workers in the Works Progress Administration (WPA) lost their jobs, and once again relief rolls swelled. Union interest in hiring black workers was placed on a back burner as Communists, busy building their united front against fascism, put less energy into persuading white workers to support the hiring of African Americans.

At a National Job March to Washington in August 1937, two black Communist leaders arrived at the tent colony and were angered by the lack of black leadership. They brought charges against a Jewish Communist, Sam Wiseman, director of the Workers Alliance in New York State.[53] Wiseman admitted that the alliance's leaders had given in to the wishes of racially prejudiced new members. He was reprimanded but continued in his post, a decision that displeased many black activists.

Black radicals were even angrier that although some white Communists had been elected to leadership roles in several unions, they did little to encourage the hiring of black workers. Only the white-collar unions "dominated by Americanized Jews of Eastern European background"[54] raised issues of importance to African Americans. In other unions, like the blue-collar Transport Workers Union, leaders were reluctant to jeopardize "white jobs" by rocking the boat. African Americans remained stuck permanently in unskilled jobs. Some black leaders, including the Reverend Adam Clayton Powell, Jr., now argued that blacks would have to fight against the companies *and* the trade unions.

Black nationalists Ira Kemp and Arthur Reid organized an all-black Harlem Labor Union. All of Harlem's jobs belonged in the hands of black workers, they said. Believing that jobs were merely a step toward building black businesses, they agitated for black employment, even at lower than standard wages. An increasing number of Harlem stores saved money by firing both black workers and white workers and replacing them with lower-paid Harlem Labor Union members.

Still refusing to launch a fight against racism in the Transport Workers Union, the disgraced radicals led a fight against racial discrimination in the utility companies where they had no union toehold. After tying up phone lines and bill-payment lines for two months, the radicals forced the two companies to open up a few clerical jobs for African Americans in

Harlem for the first time. The victory was celebrated, but the popular front never regained its former trust and credibility.[55]

In June 1938, as the revived Depression showed no signs of abating, the long awaited rematch between Joe Louis and Max Schmeling ended in a decisive victory for Louis. In several cities interracial parades took to the streets shouting out antifascist slogans. It would be one of the last joint marches for several years.

Defense contract orders began pouring into factories as American leaders could no longer ignore the war raging in Europe. Workers began returning to the production lines, this time to turn out guns, tanks, and airplanes. Few blacks were among them.

In the spring of 1939, as funding for all WPA projects was slashed even further, hunger descended like a plague on African American slums. This time there were no marches or mass meetings. By now foreign events consumed almost all the time of political activists, especially the many Jews who had fought so hard for black rights just a few years earlier. Adam Clayton Powell, Jr., commented bitterly:

> *The horrors of Europe are still being shouted from the housetops ... but nothing is being said about the plight of the Negro worker. Even my good friends down in Red Alley are strongly silent on this point, as they have been on lots of other points ... concerning the Negro workers, such as the Transport Workers Union.*[56]

Chapter

WORLD WAR II: ON THEIR OWN

The horrors in Europe were all too real. German troops marched into Austria in March 1938 with the full cooperation of Austrian Nazis. British Prime Minister Neville Chamberlain and French Prime Minister Edouard Daladier signed the Munich Pact with Hitler the following September, presenting the power-mad dictator with a piece of Czechoslovakia in exchange for his dubious promise of no further invasions.

Almost immediately the Nazis instituted a reign of terror. Thousands of Jews were arrested, their property seized. On November 9, 1938, Nazi-influenced gangs broke into Jewish-owned homes and businesses, brutally beating their occupants. The streets were filled with screams and the sound of shattering store windows. No one tried to stop the pillaging and slaughter. That night would go down in history as Kristallnacht, Night of the Broken Glass.

Raymond Geist, the American consul in Berlin, commented: "The Jews in Germany are being condemned to death and their sentence will be slowly carried out; but probably too fast for the world to save them."[1] President Roosevelt expressed his horror at the events, just as he had at lynchings, but again he took no action. In New York and other urban centers speakers at rallies demanded the lifting of the biased 1924 immigration quotas to create a safe harbor for Germany's endangered Jewish population. But public opinion polls revealed that more than three-quarters of the American people were opposed to such action.

By 1939, over a hundred hate groups existed nationally, blaming Jews for the Depression and even calling Roosevelt's New Deal the "Jew Deal." In nineteen American cities, 20,000 members of the pro-Nazi German American Bund, guided and financed by the German government, drilled in swastika-decorated uniforms.[2]

Even the plight of children did not move significant numbers of people. About 20,000 Jewish youngsters had been smuggled out of Germany and Austria and sent to other European nations after Kristallnacht. In the Senate, legislation was proposed to permit their entry into the United States, but pro-Nazi organizations raised a hue and cry. Even "solid citizens" like Laura Delano, President Roosevelt's first cousin, who was married to a high-ranking immigration commissioner, spoke out against the plan. Delano's words would go down in history: "Twenty thousand charming children would all too soon grow into 20,000 ugly adults."[3]

The Jewish quota remained firmly in place. In May 1939, a steamer named the *Saint Louis* left Germany carrying hundreds of Jewish refugees. After being turned away from Cuba, the ship sailed on to Miami. The White House was inundated with telegrams begging President Roosevelt to let the refugees in, but his answer was a firm no. The *Saint Louis* headed back to Europe with its human cargo, most of them doomed to die in the gas chambers of Nazi concentration camps.[4]

Many African American newspapers cried out against Nazi anti-Semitism,[5] frequently comparing the Nazi treatment of the European Jews with white America's treatment of African Americans.[6] But policy makers looked the other way. Throughout World War II, the already inadequate quota for Jewish immigrants was shaved down to almost nothing by bigots in the State Department. In a secret 1940 memo, American consuls abroad were instructed to postpone indefinitely the granting of visas to Jews.

With Nazi propaganda ridiculing American democracy for its treatment of minorities, black Americans hoped that now an embarrassed government would end racial segregation in the armed forces.[7] Several influential African Americans formed the

Committee for Participation of Negroes in the National Defense in 1938, demanding a change in War Department policy.

It seemed the perfect time for a reinvigorated black-Jewish alliance to fight for open doors for Jewish refugees *and* a color-blind military, but a strange turnabout occurred. On August 24, 1939, Joseph Stalin, head of the Soviet Union, signed a nonaggression pact with Adolf Hitler. A few days later Poland was invaded and occupied by German and Soviet forces. The impact on Jewish radicals was devastating. How could they explain this sudden alliance between socialists and Nazis? Earl Browder, chairman of the American Communist Party, declared that "This war is an imperialist war, and the Jewish people have nothing to gain from an Allied victory, just as they have nothing to gain from a victory by Hitler."[8]

Some Jewish Communists resigned from the Party, but others believed that the pact was a stalling technique to give the Soviet leaders time to prepare for an invasion when they would have to go it alone against "Western imperialism." Many leftists, busy defending the controversial Stalin-Hitler pact, lost interest in the struggle for military integration, weakening the black-Jewish alliance. Black leaders such as A. Philip Randolph, who had kept their criticism of the Soviet Union to a minimum during the popular-front heyday, opened a frontal assault against the Communists. As one scholar put it, "Negroes were virtually without power to do anything in America and Jews in that era had more formidable anti-Semites to contend with."[9]

On May 10, 1940, Hitler's plan for world conquest became all too clear. German troops stormed through Belgium, Holland, and Luxembourg, and broke through the French defenses, marching into Paris on June 13. The French surrendered to the German army, which now occupied two-thirds of France. England alone continued to fight Germany. German planes and rockets rained bombs down on London, setting off the Battle of Britain. British children, evacuated from war torn England, were welcomed in New York Harbor. By then many of the rejected 20,000 "charming" Jewish children were on their way to certain death in Nazi concentration camps.

As the wounded flooded into London's hospitals, the need

for blood became critical. The American Red Cross named a prominent African American scientist, Dr. Charles Drew, to head up its expanded Blood for Britain program. Dr. Drew had discovered a method for storing and using plasma as a substitute for whole blood. One morning he found an ominous memo from the War Department on his desk. It informed him that all blood was to be collected and separated according to race. Dr. Drew knew better than anyone that there were no racial differences in human blood. He also realized that the entire Red Cross program would be slowed down by the preposterous order, costing many lives. When no one in authority would listen to him, he called a press conference. He told newsmen about the ruling, calling it "insulting, immoral, and unscientific."[10] Then he publicly resigned. The foolish racist order stayed in place throughout the war.

African Americans, angry over that incident, grew angrier by the month as it became clear that the War Department's segregation policy would not change. When thirteen African American sailors, all messmen, signed a letter to a black newspaper complaining about their situation, they were booted out of the navy with dishonorable discharges. Worse yet, as government contracts poured into factories and thousands of jobs became available, very few African Americans were hired.

A. Philip Randolph had learned during the days of the popular front that only mass protest impressed politicians. He joined with other black leaders and put out a call for 10,000 black Americans to participate in a March on Washington on July 1, 1940, to demand an executive order forbidding discrimination in war plants with government contracts and in the armed forces.

Just days before the scheduled march, the media predicted that at least 50,000 people would demonstrate in Washington. President Roosevelt quickly issued Executive Order 8802, prohibiting discrimination by defense plants and in the hiring of government workers, and establishing the Fair Employment Practices Commission (FEPC) to enforce his order. President Roosevelt sidestepped the issue of military integration by issuing a vague statement about equal treatment. Randolph now faced a serious dilemma. The question of military integration was a moral issue, but jobs meant survival. Plans for the march were postponed indefinitely.

Americans followed the events overseas with growing alarm.[11] German air raids over England and Scotland intensified, and German submarines attacked convoys of U.S. merchant ships loaded with supplies bound for Britain. President Roosevelt sent warships to protect the convoys. Advised that there had not been enough volunteers to bring the armed forces up to full strength, Roosevelt proposed legislation for an immediate draft.

African American leaders pressed for guarantees of equality in the new draft law. Eleanor Roosevelt convinced her husband to meet with a few black leaders, including Walter White of the NAACP and A. Philip Randolph. Also attending the meeting were Secretary of the Navy Frank Knox and Assistant Secretary of War Robert P. Patterson. Both refused to give an inch. President Roosevelt promised he would attempt to figure out ways to lessen discrimination, but he did not disagree with Knox's insistence that close living conditions on naval vessels made integration impossible. He asked the War Department to issue an ameliorating statement,[12] none of which appeared in the draft law he signed.

The Republicans hammered away at the issue. In October, a number of hasty appointments were announced by the White House. An African American colonel, Benjamin O. Davis, was promoted to the rank of general, the first of his race; a black adviser to the director of selective service was named; and William H. Hastie was named assistant to the Secretary of War Henry Stimson.[13] In his diary, Stimson complained, "The Negroes are taking advantage of this period just before election to try to get everything they can in the way of recognition from the Army."[14]

One black general and two advisers did not impress very many African Americans. Although the majority of African Americans and Jewish Americans cast their votes for Roosevelt again, they did so in lesser numbers than in 1936.

President Roosevelt started his third term in office with his military leaders satisfied that the status quo had been maintained and his state department officials continuing to close the doors to Jewish refugees. But the battle was far from over. The glaring contradiction of black men fighting in a segregated military against an enemy proclaiming the superiority of the Aryan race was obvious to too many people.

Before the United States entered the war, racist officials attempted to lower the number of African Americans inducted into the army by ordering higher literacy standards in the hope of screening out many potential black draftees from the South. Secretary of War Stimson retracted the order when he noticed it also banned "some very good and illiterate [white] recruits from the southern mountain states."[15]

Stimson, who liked to boast in public that some of his ancestors were abolitionists, wrote in his diary that leaders who wanted integration were actually seeking "social equality"; he also worried about "race mixture by marriage." He concluded that "In the draft we are preparing to give the negroes a fair shot in every service . . . but I hope for heaven's sake they won't mix the white and colored troops together . . . for then we shall certainly have trouble."[16]

Stimson's private opinion reflected the attitude of most military officers. The nation's leaders called the United States "the last bulwark of democracy," but African Americans willing to risk their lives to defend democracy were turned away from every branch of the military. Since the Fair Employment Practices Commission had almost no enforcement power, many defense plants, called "arsenals of democracy," refused to accept black applicants for their training programs. African American blood donors were also turned away after being told that the Red Cross had enough Negro blood. Draft boards responsible for inducting black Americans were almost always lily white. Even many air-raid shelters were segregated. For Mississippi's segregated schools the state legislature passed a law requiring all references to democracy and elections "to be excluded from the Negroes' textbooks."[17]

Black draftees were usually assigned to lowly service units with high-sounding names like the Engineers Corp or Quartermaster Corps. In the Air Force, segregated African American units were given names like "aviation squadrons" and "aviation quartermaster truck companies," as men who had dreamed of piloting planes performed cleanup and delivery chores on air bases.

During the First World War, most African Americans had gone along with W. E. B. Du Bois, agreeing to hold off on demands for equality at home until the war ended. Now every major black-owned newspaper and organization believed that African Americans had to fight immediately on two fronts— democracy abroad *and* democracy at home. As a large letter *V* for "Victory" became a popular wartime symbol, African Americans converted it into a double V—one *V* for victory in the war and the other for victory over racism at home.

William Hastie quickly learned that he was powerless to do much of anything in his new job as Stimson's adviser. In 1941, after white military police killed two black soldiers, Hastie asked the War Department to issue a press release condemning racism in the military. Army commanders instead blamed the black newspapers for publicizing the incident! By the end of the year, few black men believed that they had the slightest chance of fair treatment in the military.

As war preparations speeded up, isolationists still tried to prevent America's involvement in the conflict. The U.S. ambassador to England, Joseph P. Kennedy, the father of future president John F. Kennedy, met with Hollywood studio executives and asked them to stop making anti-Nazi films. Such movies endangered peace, he insisted. Kennedy claimed that the British, with German bombs raining down on their heads, were blaming the Jews for their ordeal. Actually, with the exception of Charlie Chaplin's *The Great Dictator*, which satirized Adolf Hitler, no anti-Nazi films had been produced. Shortly after Kennedy's visit, a Senate subcommittee came to Hollywood to investigate the same question of anti-Nazi filmmaking and supposed "violations of American neutrality." Before the investigation could gather steam, though, America was at war and anti-Nazi films became a high priority.

In June 1941, German tanks quickly gobbled up hundreds of miles of Soviet territory. Communists around the world protested the invasion. World War II was no longer just an "imperialist war." Now leftists joined thousands of antifascists in the United States and England in urging Roosevelt and Churchill to immediately stop the Nazis.

As German troops captured Soviet cities and towns, they seized and murdered half a million Russian Jews, labeling them as political enemies and "undesirables."

On December 7, 1941, a black sailor named Dorie Miller was busy setting tables and preparing food with other African American messmen deep in a battleship berthed at the U.S. naval base at Pearl Harbor, Hawaii. Suddenly the men heard the ominous sound of bombs exploding far above their heads. The messmen had received very little weapons training, but Miller did not stop to think about that. He raced topside and saw Japanese planes bombing and strafing the many ships berthed in the area and men falling dead all around him. Pointing an anti-aerial gun toward the sky, he fired away until three Japanese bombers crashed into the sea. Dorie Miller received the Navy Cross for bravery, but was never allowed to advance past his messman's rank.

Within hours after the bombing of Pearl Harbor, Congress declared war on Japan. Three days later, Japan's allies, Germany and Italy, declared war on the United States. Americans huddled anxiously around their radios and heard how the Japanese were capturing Pacific islands and winning control over Southeast Asia while the Nazis swallowed up more Soviet territory. Allied troops were bogged down in fierce desert battles against the Germans in North Africa.

With World War II spreading out on several fronts, thousands of men were desperately needed to replace the dead and wounded. Yet black soldiers, stationed near battle areas and more than willing to fight, were not brought forward.[18]

Stimson, finding it difficult to place all black draftees in the army, asked Roosevelt to order the navy to change its policy. Roosevelt consulted with Knox, who, in a macabre statement, told the president that

> *the white man ... considers himself of a superior race and will not admit the Negro to intimate family relationships leading to marriage. These concepts may not be truly democratic, but it is doubtful if the most ardent*

lovers of democracy will dispute them, particularly in regard to intermarriage.[19]

Under pressure from black leaders, Roosevelt finally persuaded Knox to announce in 1942 that 14,000 African American men would be permitted to enlist for "general service" in the next year.

Meanwhile, Hastie stepped up his efforts to force army authorities to assign African American soldiers to combat units in the same ratio as whites. He asked Stimson to present a plan to General George Marshall, army chief of staff, wherein small black units would be assigned to large white units. Marshall's answer was that "Experiments within the army in the solution of social problems are fraught with danger to efficiency, discipline, and morale."[20]

At army bases, black soldiers, who had been trained for combat, were assigned to fight fires, do landscape work, and move furniture and supplies. A field commander told General Dwight D. Eisenhower that blacks were kept in such assignments "due to the inherent psychology of the colored race."[21] Even in the Medical Corps, almost all black men were assigned to sanitation companies, digging graves and latrines. There were *no* white sanitation companies.

In response to growing protests, the War Department created four new black infantry divisions, each one with 15,000 men, and announced they would soon be active. "Soon" turned out to be a long way off. The Army General Staff had great difficulty figuring out where to send the men for training. Most army camps were in the South, where segregationist laws meant that black soldiers had to be stationed on separate bases. A southern governors conference voted unanimously in 1942 to oppose the stationing of black soldiers in their states. The reaction in other parts of the nation was also racist.[22]

The vast majority of black soldiers were eventually stationed in segregated sections of southern training camps. On leave in nearby communities, they were frequently insulted, beaten, and even hanged or shot.[23] Those few selected for officers' training lived in near isolation at supposedly integrated installations. At Camp Wheeler, Georgia, for example, the only black officer candidate lived alone in a two-story apartment building and ate alone in a marked-off corner in the officers' mess hall. When African American officers graduated, they were assigned to work under the command of white officers, many of whom were openly racist. A few blacks ultimately resigned their commissions. One described the "humiliations" and "insults" as "mounted one upon another until one's zest is chilled and spirit broken."[24]

Jewish men were integrated into all branches of the armed services but many faced undisguised anti-Semitism. A marine corporal, two years in service, wrote home: "I am the only Jewish boy in this detachment. I am confronted with anti-Semitism on all sides. Sorry I got into this outfit."[25]

Although the proportion of Jews serving in the armed forces was far greater than their percentage in the population, lies were spread that Jewish men avoided military service and raked in war profits at home while Christian men died in battle. Serving in the armed forces were 550,000 Jewish Americans, of whom 40,000 were wounded, 11,000 died in battle, and 52,000 were decorated.[26]

A strange contradiction prevailed all during World War II. While Americans were fighting overseas to defeat the world's leading racists, at home racism and anti-Semitism actually reached new heights! For example, almost immediately after Pearl Harbor, President Roosevelt signed Executive Order 9066, authorizing the army to seize all 110,000 Japanese Americans on the West Coast and remove them to detention camps. Hardly any pro-Nazi Germans were detained. A number of black organizations protested the obvious racism.[27]

Anti-Semitism escalated. Polls taken by public opinion expert Elmo Roper in 1942 revealed that the majority of Americans believed that Jews were more of a threat than any other group except the Japanese! Church authorities ordered Father Coughlin to censor his anti-Semitic remarks, but a pro-Coughlin group, the International Catholic Truth Society, was permitted to spew out thousands of anti-Semitic tracts. Gerald L. K. Smith and other fundamentalist preachers also agitated against Jews freely. Their diatribes inspired many acts of anti-Semitic violence.

Boston, where Jewish cemeteries and synagogues were defiled with swastikas, became a strong center of fascist supporters. A gang of twenty young men severely beat three Jewish children. An investigation by the Massachusetts governor fixed blame on the "laxity and inaction" of the police. In the Midwest, a pro-Nazi gang grabbed a twelve-year-old boy and held him down while they painted a Star of David and the word "Jude," German for "Jew," on his chest.

A high school teacher in Texas learned that his former pupil Arthur Berkman had been killed in action. He wrote a letter to the *Houston Chronicle*:

> *Arthur was sweet and decent and considerate and helpful.... The next time I hear the slightest remark about the Jewish people I am going to say, "Arthur Berkman, an American, of the Jewish faith died for you. I wonder at your pride and arrogance." Arthur wouldn't have said that, though. He probably would have said, "Father, forgive them, they know not what they do."* [28]

Congress, the State Department, the Supreme Court—all had the power to challenge wartime racism but instead they legalized it. In Congress, one of the worst offenders was John Rankin, a Democrat from Mississippi. He referred to a Jewish newsman as "that little kike." Worse, he blocked special legislation to permit the entry into the United States of a Jewish refugee couple and their daughter. Two of the couple's sons were in the U.S. Army, about to be shipped overseas to fight! Minutes after delivering a passionate speech in response to one of Rankin's racist outbursts, Congressman M. Michael Edelstein of New York died of a heart attack. [29]

According to Adam Clayton Powell, Jr., who in 1944 became the first African American elected from Harlem to the House of Representatives, right-wing groups failed dismally in their efforts to attract African Americans to the anti-Semitic cause. [30] A tiny group of black nationalists continued their street-corner harangues against Jewish shopkeepers and landlords; a handful of anti-Jewish editorials appeared in a very few black newspapers; and one short-lived blatantly pro-Hitler publication, *Dynamite*, openly stated its admiration for Adolf Hitler. But otherwise, blacks knew better. The Jewish press continued to publicize discrimination against African Americans.

In 1941–1942, vans equipped with poison gas tanks were set up at Chelmno, Poland. Jews were lined up at gunpoint and forced to file ninety at a time into the death vans. Seven hundred thousand were exterminated. Hundreds of thousands more were herded into the Warsaw ghetto, from where they were shipped to death camps like Auschwitz. The mayor of the Warsaw ghetto, Adam Caerniakow, killed himself rather than follow the Nazis' orders to select the victims. The U.S. press scarcely mentioned these developments, and years later many Americans would say that they found the reported barbaric behavior of the Nazis impossible to believe.

In German-occupied France, with Vichy French citizens assisting them, the Germans parked buses in front of apartment house entrances, pulled Jewish occupants out of their homes, loaded them into the vehicles, and carted them off to detention camps for future shipment to Polish gas chambers. Risking their own lives, French Resistance supporters managed to hide about eight thousand children. U.S. officials condemned the Nazi actions, but took no steps to rescue the doomed refugees. Eleanor Roosevelt tried to help get immigration visas for about five thousand children, only to fail when the Vichy government claimed that they did not want to separate the children from their parents!

The doors to America remained shut year after year. Despite poor press coverage, the whole world was learning about the genocide. Memorials for the growing numbers of exterminated Jews were held in several U.S. cities. On July 21, 1942, a protest rally was conducted at New York's Madison Square Garden. Twenty thousand attended, and thousands more stood outside. They heard heartrending speeches by Rabbi Stephen Wise, Governor Herbert Lehman, Mayor Fiorello La Guardia, Methodist bishop Francis McConnell, William Green of the AFL, and A. Philip Randolph. "No Negro is secure from intolerance and race prejudice so long as one Jew is a victim of anti-Semitism," Randolph intoned.[31] President Roosevelt sent a message to the meeting promising punishment of the Nazi murderers *after* the war.

By August 1942 the Allied military situation had improved somewhat, but it was obvious that if the U.S. government waited for the war to be won, there would be few Jews left to save. Throughout the spring and summer thousands of sealed railroad cars rumbled through Europe, headed east. Stephen Wise, a personal friend of President Roosevelt and the leading rabbi in the United States, told a friend, "I am almost demented over my people's grief."[32] The State Department asked Wise to keep silent until the stories could be checked. Four months later, the worst news was confirmed. By then two million more Jews had been murdered.

At several black colleges in the South, Jewish refugee scholars followed the reports from Europe. Viewed with deep hostility by the townspeople, most of these professors refused to patronize segregated town facilities, instead socializing with their black colleagues. Some of them endured poison pen letters and even bomb threats from local racists. After the war, German Jewish sociologist Ernest Borinski was sometimes asked by students and faculty members at Tougaloo College in Mississippi about the fate of his family who were stranded in Germany during the war and unable to obtain visas. "I will not speak of family," he answered. "I have liquidated this area for my mental health." But he was quick to speak out about a local Mississippi board of education article on a "conspiracy of Satan and the Jews" aimed at freeing blacks, comparing the piece to Nazi propaganda.[33]

African Americans, embroiled in their own losing struggle with the military, nevertheless made their views known on the plight of the Jews. On February 23, 1943, the NAACP executive committee pledged "its unqualified and unlimited effort in behalf of the persecuted Jews of the world, which includes anti-Semitism in the United States as well as mass slaughter in Poland." It said the "cold-blooded campaign of extermination of the Jews" had no "parallels in the history of the world."[34]

By the spring of 1943, out of half a million black men in the army, only 79,000 were stationed overseas. They were anxious to fight. But several black combat units were downgraded into service units at the very moment the army high command was complaining about troop shortages!

In England, where thousands of black soldiers were waiting out the war, many British citizens treated them as equals. Some white American soldiers spread wild stories that the blacks were rapists with tails. General Eisenhower, commander in the European theater of war, issued orders forbidding such slander, but the situation deteriorated when *Life* magazine published a photograph of black soldiers dancing with white Englishwomen. White American soldiers threatened to boycott any public place that allowed integrated couples on its premises. Fearful of losing business, some places barred blacks.

In August 1942, a federal Advisory Committee on Negro Troop Policy was formed, but William Hastie was excluded from its meetings. Five months later, when the army air force announced its plan to set up a segregated officers' candidate school for black airmen, Hastie resigned and called a press conference. He revealed the real attitude of the top brass, telling the assembled reporters how one white officer had said that the all-black Ninety-ninth Pursuit Squadron existed only to provide a place for African Americans and how black men were still not permitted to fight. Public protest finally forced the army air force to send the squadron to North Africa under the command of Colonel Benjamin O. Davis, Jr., General Davis's son. There the commander of the Fifth Air Force kept the fliers sitting around for months.

During the hot summer of 1943, race riots broke out in dozens of cities.[35] In Mobile, Alabama, when a dozen black men were promoted to welding jobs at a shipbuilding company, 20,000 workers left their workstations and rioted for four days, beating up black men and women. Troops had to be called in to restore calm. In Beaumont, Texas, a rape rumor caused a riot that leveled a black neighborhood.[36]

Perhaps the worst troubles occurred in Detroit, where a year earlier a white mob had violently attacked black families who were moving into a government housing project for black defense workers.[37] A federal investigation had found the Detroit police complicitous in "suppressing the Negroes."[38] The leadership of the United Auto Workers (UAW), which included many Jewish workers, repeatedly protested acts of white racism. On April 11, 1943, a joint UAW-NAACP rally of 5,000 people took place in Detroit's main square to demand the hiring of African American men and women. But the white workers at the rally were far from a majority in the union. Just two months later, when three black men were promoted at the Packard plant, about 25,000 workers conducted a work stoppage to protest. White workers claimed they were concerned that black workers would take their jobs when the war ended. Some of them belonged to a group close to the Ku Klux Klan known as the National Workers League.[39]

Then, on the hot and humid evening of June 20, 1943, Belle Isle, a small island park in the Detroit River, was filled with 100,000 people, many of them African Americans from Paradise Valley, a nearby black ghetto. A scuffle between white and black youths quickly escalated into several days of violence. White mobs raced through Detroit, stopping streetcars and pulling off black riders, and looting and burning. Four white youths shot and killed a fifty-nine-year-old black man, saying they had done it "for the hell of it." The following night the governor of Michigan called President Roosevelt and asked for federal troops to put down the riots. By then twenty-five African Americans and nine whites lay dead, hundreds were wounded, and Detroit's shopping district lay in ruins. Seventeen of the twenty-five black dead had been killed by police. When newspaper photos showed a policeman holding an injured black by both arms while a white rioter struck him in the face, anger swept through black communities across the nation—anger at the slow progress of blacks in obtaining war plant jobs, anger at the nation's refusal to allow black soldiers to fight in the war, anger at the rising tide of racism.[40]

The Germans and Japanese chortled with delight over the problems of American "democracy." A Radio Tokyo broadcaster commented that "supposedly civilized Americans . . . deny the Negroes the opportunity to engage in respectable jobs, the right of access to restaurants, theaters, or the same train accommodations as themselves, and periodically will run amok to lynch Negroes individually or to slaughter them wholesale."[41]

In the midst of the horror in Detroit, many white people

did their best to end the violence. The CIO managed to keep the war plants operating all during the riots. Adam Clayton Powell, Jr., who was in Detroit during the disturbances, later described some heartening scenes:

> *The first was two soldiers ... helping a beaten black man and defying the mob which was surging around them. The next, two sailors walking into a crowd of over a hundred and protesting the stoning to death of a black man. . . . The ringleader said to them, "What's this to you?" One of the sailors replied, "I'll tell you what it is to me. One of this boy's race was on my ship at Pearl Harbor and when the ship was sinking and the captain was injured he came from out of the mess room, crawled across the deck, rescued the captain and went back to an anti-aircraft gun ... and personally manned that gun until the ammunition was exhausted."*[42]

City governments rushed to take steps to avoid similar disturbances. New York Mayor La Guardia announced, "I will not permit ... any minority group to be abused by another group."[43] But on Sunday, August 1, a scuffle between a black soldier and a policeman in Harlem concluded with the shooting and wounding of the soldier. Rumors flew, and "the citizens went on a rampage, not because of that one isolated rumor," Powell later insisted, "but because before them there rose up the whole sorrowful, disgraceful, bloody record of America's treatment of one million blacks in uniform." Calling the episode "Civil War II," Powell said "the Harlem outbreak was not a race riot."[44] The mayor himself came to the area with two black leaders to appeal for peace. He called for 1,500 mostly black civilian volunteers to join with 5,000 regular police. About twenty-four hours later, five black men lay dead and property loss exceeded $5 million.[45]

The struggle to open America's doors wider to Jewish refugees fared no better than the fight for black equality. As the mass murder of Jews in concentration camps—Hitler's "final solution"—escalated, pressure was applied on Congress to form a special rescue agency. Then Henry Morgenthau, the

The Jewish community in Lublin, Poland.
The people of this community, like all others
under the Nazis, were annihilated in
the concentration camps.

Roosevelt-appointed secretary of the Treasury, uncovered a shocking scandal. A special license required to pay Hitler a ransom for the lives of 70,000 Romanian Jews had been deliberately held up by bureaucrats. Rabbi Stephen Wise and other Jewish leaders had raised the necessary money. Morgenthau protested directly to President Roosevelt. To avoid an almost certain scandal, Roosevelt issued Executive Order 9417, directly ordering the formation of the War Refugee Board. But all told, most of the board's efforts were too little and too late. By then, almost six million Jews had been methodically murdered, and a tiny remnant of barely surviving victims waited in the camps praying for rescue.[46]

In 1944, the war began to turn in favor of the Allies.[47] Still, black soldiers waited to become part of the final onslaught to defeat the Axis powers (Germany and Japan—Italy had capitulated in October 1943). Stimson started an uproar by announcing that the combat-ready all-black Second Cavalry Division was about to be downgraded into a service group. Pressed to explain his decision, Stimson responded that the men were "unable to master efficiently the techniques of modern weapons." Headlines in the black press blared out the news that Stimson believed that black soldiers were too dumb to fight.

With elections less than a year away, Roosevelt asked the Coast Guard and Marine Corps to open their doors to black recruits. Both branches of the service stalled or refused outright. When Secretary of the Navy Knox died, James Forrestal, a liberal, assumed his post. Forrestal immediately appointed African American Lester Granger, former secretary of the National Urban League, as his aide. In a short time, two all-black antisubmarine vessels were sent to sea and the crews of twenty-five ships were peacefully integrated.

By the spring of 1944, a bold plan was in the works to end the war. A second front would be opened by American and British armies invading France in order to trap Nazi forces in a pincer between them and the Soviet (Red) Army pushing in from the east. On June 6, 1944, D Day, this second front opened when 185,000 Allied troops landed on the beaches of Normandy, France. Five hundred African Americans of the 320th Barrage Balloon Battalion launched huge balloons over the heads of the landing forces to hide them from German bombers.

In one of the landing barges, as bullets sprayed all around them, a Jewish soldier, Harry Rosenzweig, was shocked to hear one of his comrades loudly curse, "Damn the Jews! We're in this mess because of the lousy kikes!"[48]

A few black combat groups were at last allowed to see some action. In the skies over Italy, the men of the Ninety-ninth Pursuit Squadron, calling themselves the Lonely Eagles, shot down several German planes. The Ninety-second Infantry Division fought alongside the Fifth Army in Italy and won many medals in six months of heavy battle. A section of the Ninety-third was sent to the Pacific, mainly for mop-up operations.

About seven hundred black fighters of the 762nd Division, the first all-black tank battalion in history, were shipped across the Atlantic. Segregated from white troops, they stayed in the bottom of the vessel for the three-week journey.[49] Then, fighting their way across Europe, they rode over land mines and booby traps, protecting the white infantry units marching behind them.[50]

In mid-December they rolled toward Belgium, where a terrible battle was in progress. The Germans had broken through Allied lines. The Battle of the Bulge, Germany's last desperate offensive, had begun. The 762nd won a victory in four-foot-deep snow as they broke through to join the battle.

With thousands of men killed or wounded, the call for replacements grew more desperate and the old cry for an integrated volunteer unit grew louder. Eisenhower agreed to allow black volunteers to form *segregated* units fighting *alongside* white companies. More than five thousand men volunteered, and twenty-five hundred were accepted and trained for six weeks. It was impossible, of course, to maintain segregation under fire. Before the battle, two-thirds of the white soldiers had supported segregation of the military. After fighting side by side with black soldiers, two-thirds backed integration. General Benjamin O. Davis wanted the army to publicize these findings, but instead silence was maintained and the black soldiers were returned to their service units.

Even after U.S. soldiers had their first glimpse of the horrors inside of the Nazi concentration camps, anti-Semitism persisted. A Jewish-American Red Cross staff member remembered stopping at a U.S. Military Government office in Magdeburg, Germany, to get directions to a refugee camp. She was anxious to offer her help to almost three thousand survivors of the concentration camp at Bergen-Belsen. The Nazis had locked their captives in railroad cars as they fled, and they had remained there for ten days before American soldiers found them. The Red Cross worker recalled that

> *Major A said to me "Oh, you want to visit our kikes; be careful or they'll take everything you've got."... Major S said, "So you want to visit our long-noses," pulling his nose. "Maybe you can cut down their noses to the size of some of the parts the Nazis cut off."*[51]

The officers were not an exception. None other than General George Patton, even after viewing the nightmare scene at Buchenwald concentration camp, remained an ardent racist. Later he called the Germans "the only decent people in Europe" and said the problem rested with "the Jews. . . . Everyone believes that the displaced person is a human being, which he is not, and this applies particularly to the Jews who are lower than animals."[52]

President Roosevelt died on April 12, 1945, just weeks before Paul Parks and his men entered Dachau. Germany surrendered on May 7. Adolf Hitler committed suicide in an underground bunker as Russian troops closed in. In August, after the new president, Harry S. Truman, ordered the atomic bombing of two Japanese cities, Hiroshima and Nagasaki, Japan also surrendered.

African American servicemen returned home determined to wipe out the homegrown version of the prejudice and racism that had almost destroyed the world. Having helped to save democracy, they now intended to make democracy a reality.

Chapter

THE COLD WAR VERSUS CIVIL RIGHTS

Racial tension ratcheted up another notch when the determined black veterans returned home.[1] In the chamber of the U.S. Senate, Senator Theodore Bilbo of Mississippi proclaimed: "Red-blooded Anglo-Saxon men should stop Negroes from attempting to vote by any means."[2] These threatening words were quickly followed by deeds. Assaults on black veterans broke out in many cities. In February 1946, police permanently blinded a black veteran, Sergeant Isaac Woodard, Jr., still in uniform, when they dragged him from a bus in South Carolina, beat him with blackjacks, and twisted their nightsticks into his eyes.

President Truman had called for freedom throughout the world, yet in the United States racist violence was out of control. Thirteen million African Americans were determined to call a halt to it and ban poll taxes, lynchings, and job and housing discrimination. Membership in the NAACP skyrocketed from over 50,000 in 1940 to 351,000 in 1945.[3]

Most black leaders knew full well that without white allies they would be fighting a losing battle. Prominent among the whites who seemed concerned were Jewish Americans. The nightmare of the Holocaust had an enormous impact even on those Jews who had never been political activists in the prewar days. Many believed that what had happened in Germany could happen anywhere. They realized that in a nation that legalized racism against blacks, Jews were not safe either. One writer stated that the Holocaust "shaped the Jewish vision as

113

ally to the underdog."[4] Another noted that a broad new informal alliance formed between "the major groups usually called racial minorities. Jews . . . played a key role in sparking the [new] informal civil-rights coalition."[5]

All over the nation, interracial and interfaith conferences were held. Jewish magazines published articles about injustices against black Americans. African Americans wrote about the horrors caused by anti-Semitism. Court cases often became joint enterprises as lawyers and fund-raisers from Jewish groups pitched in with the NAACP and Latino organizatons to attempt to reverse segregation in public places.[6]

A major goal of this postwar alliance was to keep the wartime Fair Employment Practices Commission (FEPC) alive. Despite its lack of strong enforcement regulations, the FEPC had helped members of all the minorities find better paying work in war plants. A "Save the FEPC" rally was held in New York City in June 1945, but southern Democrats and conservative Republicans banded together in Congress to defeat a proposal by liberal Democrats for the agency's temporary extension. The final FEPC report presented the sad news that the "wartime gains of Negro, Mexican-American, and Jewish workers are being dissipated through an unchecked revival of discriminatory practices."[7]

President Truman angrily denounced the anti-FEPC legislators and appointed William H. Hastie governor of the Virgin Islands, a majority-black U.S. possession. This sequence of events became a familiar pattern: proposals by liberals; defeat by southern Democrats and conservative Republicans; and then the appointment of a few African Americans. But Truman assured FEPC advocates that there would be no discriminatory hiring for civil service jobs or government contract work during his presidency. President Truman kept his word, but there were few new civil service jobs and most defense plants had cut down their workforces.

As efforts to achieve equal rights bogged down, opponents of civil rights unleashed a new weapon: anticommunism." Over the next decade and a half, a modern witch-hunt, ostensibly for Communist Party members in the United States, often labeled "McCarthyism," intimidated and silenced almost all the leaders and participants in the renewed struggle for justice: union and civil rights activists, teachers who emphasized democratic values, filmmakers who pierced the Hollywood tinsel shield, authors who dared to write about social ills, restaurant workers, sanitation workers, seamstresses, and millions of ordinary people who were anxious to turn the nightmare of racism into the dream of equality.

There were other reasons for beating the anticommunist drums of the "Cold War" between the United States and the Soviet Union. For one thing, strikes could be prevented and wages held down by accusing union leaders of being agents of a foreign power. For another, economists knew that it was armaments production that had finally pulled the nation out of the Great Depression. They feared that if the war plants closed, the economy would stall again. To rationalize continued defense production, a potential enemy had to be created. It was not easy to convince most Americans that the Soviet Union posed a threat to the United States. After all, the Soviet economy was in ruins and 20 million Soviet citizens had died in the war fighting on the U.S. side.

But a window of opportunity opened, providing a pretext to stir up fears about a possible "Soviet Communist takeover of the world." In Africa, the Middle East, and Asia, people who had been ruled by colonial masters before the war were winning their independence. In former dictatorships of Europe and Latin America, antifascist forces were carrying out campaigns for democracy and improved wages that had strong popular support. Immediately, British and American leaders labeled the anticolonial and pro-democratic struggles "Communist."[8] The cry went out that the Communists were seeking world conquest, just as Hitler had done. Any American supporting these struggles was called disloyal and un-American—a Communist sympathizer, a pinko or a Red.

It was not that easy, however, to pin the Communist label on every black, Asian, Hispanic, Indian, and Jew who demanded equal rights. All during the summer and fall of 1946 a strong united response to racist violence moved into high gear. A delegation from the Black National Newspaper Publishers Association met with President Truman demanding an antilynching law. Four hundred members of the National Association of Colored Women marched in front of the White House also urging presidential action. Protest meetings and rallies drew large racially mixed crowds. Representatives of forty different human rights and civil rights organizations formed the National Emergency Committee against Mob Violence and met with the president. Walter White told the story of the blinding of Isaac Woodard. "My God! I had no idea that it was as terrible as that! We've got to do something!" Truman exclaimed.[9]

With newspapers in the Soviet Union reporting on racist incidents in the "free world," the president issued Executive Order 9808, creating the president's Committee on Civil Rights. The committee was instructed to find "ways to safeguard the civil rights of the people."[10] About eight months later, the commission submitted its draft report, entitled *To Secure These Rights*, proposing a full range of new civil rights legislation. The report emphasized the reaction overseas:

> *We cannot escape the fact that our civil rights record has been an issue in world politics.... They have tried to prove our democracy an empty fraud, and our nation a consistent oppressor of underprivileged people.*[11]

Members of the civil rights alliance were unimpressed by the legislation proposed by the committee, a method that had been tried unsuccessfully for years. There was little reason to expect Congress to have a change of heart unless people initiated direct actions to secure these rights, as they had done in the 1930s.

The first issue the civil rights coalition tackled was an old one: military segregation. That was something, after all, that could be ended by a presidential executive order, bypassing Congress. With rising postwar unemployment among African Americans, many young black men had rushed to join the peacetime military. When their numbers reached 16 percent in the army, recruitment of blacks was suspended. Pressure mounted to drop the quota system and integrate the military. Chief of Staff George C. Marshall established the Gillem Board to study the issue, then recommended a go-slow approach of placing small black units within white ones. An editorial in the *Amsterdam News* reflected civil rights advocates' reaction to the board's plan:"All it did was to slice Jim Crow a little thinner and spread it around more so it wouldn't make such a stinkin' heap in the middle of the national floor."[12]

As anticipated, Congress did nothing. Adam Clayton Powell, Jr., proposed several bills including a new permanent Fair Employment Practice Commission proposal. Republican House Speaker Joseph Martin candidly admitted that "industrialists are the Republicans' chief supporters so we won't pass FEPC."[13] President Truman made only passing mention of civil rights in his State of the Union address, but he appointed the liberal Forrestal as secretary of defense. By then, more than seven hundred organizations belonged to the expanded civil rights coalition.

In response to the government's failure to act, some activists decided to turn for help to the international community. W. E. B. Du Bois and others wrote "An Appeal to the World," listing the grievances of black Americans, and presented it to the Human Rights Commission of the United Nations. U.S. government officials were mortified. When the Universal Declaration of Human Rights was adopted by the UN General Assembly in 1948, in order to spare the world's most powerful nation embarrassment it contained no specific reference to racism in the United States.

Nonetheless, chipping away state by state, the civil rights alliance won a few changes here and there.[14] The vast majority of African Americans were unaware of the snail's-pace progress. They were stuck in low-paid unskilled jobs, and they faced frequent unemployment. Many did follow sports developments, however, especially baseball, and they were thrilled when Jackie Robinson became the first black player on a major league team.

Under pressure from some fans and the Committee to End Jim Crow in Baseball, club owners met in 1946 and voted 15-1 against bringing in African American players. Branch Rickey, the manager of the Brooklyn Dodgers, cast the sole yes vote. He had already signed Jackie Robinson to a minor league contract and planned to make him a member of the Dodgers in 1947.

Before his first game, Robinson was warned by Rickey that he would probably be abused by the fans. Instead, the abuse came from some of his teammates, who petitioned Rickey to exclude Robinson. Before spring training in 1947, Rickey met with a few local black clergymen and asked them to persuade black fans to behave calmly during games. As it turned out, African Americans were not the only overjoyed spectators.

Years later, a Jewish New Yorker, Joel Oppenheimer, told writer Jonathan Kaufman about a game he attended at Ebbets Field, Brooklyn, in 1947:

> *During the game Jackie made a good play in the field, at which point everyone was yelling, "Jackie, Jackie, Jackie," and I was yelling with them. And suddenly I realized that behind me someone was yelling, "Yonkel, Yonkel, Yonkel," which is Yiddish for Jackie. I realized that here was the only white face in a crowd of blacks aside from me, and he's yelling, "Yonkel, Yonkel, Yonkel." It was a very moving moment.* [15]

By 1950, only eleven more black players had been contracted by major league teams, all of them hired by the Dodgers or the Cleveland Indians. The New York Yankees made no move to change their policy until 1954. Every Saturday pickets, many of them Jewish, lined up near the ticket windows of Yankee Stadium, chanting over and over "Jim Crow must go."

A few Jewish ballplayers had been playing in the major leagues long before Robinson joined the Dodgers. According to the best-known Jewish player, Hank Greenberg, they experienced considerable anti-Semitism but nothing compared with the treatment Robinson received.[16] Greenberg remembered that:

> *Jackie had it tough, tougher than any ballplayer who ever lived. I happened to be a Jew, one of the few in baseball, but I was white, and I didn't have horns like some had thought I did. Jo-Jo White had said to me, "I thought all you Jews had horns on your head." But I identified with Jackie Robinson, I had feelings for him because they had treat-*

ed me the same way. Not as bad. . . . I said to Robinson
at first base, "Don't pay any attention to these southern
[bench] jockeys. They aren't worth anything as far as
you're concerned." He thanked me and I said, "Would you
like to go to dinner?" He said, "I'd love to go to dinner, but
I shouldn't because it'll put you on the spot."[17]

Pride over black baseball players, however, could not erase terrible problems like housing. Even the few African Americans
with improved incomes had difficulty escaping from the ghettos. Landlords in other neighborhoods routinely claimed apartments had already been rented whenever African Americans
appeared. All veterans had been promised low-interest government loans for home purchases, and thousands of inexpensive
houses were built in suburbs of large and small cities. Most of
the deeds contained "restrictive covenants"—clauses that for-
bade sale to racial minorities.

The report of the President's Committee on Civil Rights
had called for an end to such covenants. In 1947, a dozen coali-
tions filed suits challenging them. While the cases slowly made
their way through the courts, black families remained stuck in
segregated slums.

Meanwhile, the NAACP and Jewish organizations decided
to put more pressure on Hollywood producers to make
antiracist films. Film reviewers in the NAACP publication the
Crisis had criticized Walt Disney's *Song of the South* in 1946.
They referred to the storytelling black Uncle Remus of the film
as an "Uncle Tom-Aunt Jemima caricature complete with all the
fawning standard equipment thereof—the toothy smile, battered hat, gray beard, and a profusion of 'dis' and 'dat' talk . . .
[that] has done more to . . . set back Negro progress than a fist-
ful of Bilbo speeches."[18]

They threatened to organize boycotts of films containing
shuffling, eye-rolling Negroes and vulgar Jews speaking with a
thick accent. Some Jewish film producers had visited Nazi concentration camps and returned shocked and horrified. They
decided to make some "social problem" films. Since some
wartime films had portrayed Nazi mistreatment of Jews, anti-
Semitism seemed a less controversial topic to start with than

whites' abuse of blacks. Although Hollywood's leading rabbi, Edgar Magnin, warned the producers that such films might whip the anti-Semites into a frenzy, a few were produced. One, made by Darryl Zanuck, a Protestant from Nebraska with a deep hatred of prejudice, won the 1947 Oscar for Best Picture: *Gentleman's Agreement*. Black film critics promptly praised the film and suggested that Hollywood do the same for African Americans.

By 1949 a number of films were carrying openly antiracist messages to the nation's moviegoers.[19] "The handkerchief was snatched off," Walter White happily wrote in the *Crisis*. "Hollywood can never go back to its portrayal of colored people as witless menials or idiotic buffoons."[20]

The new trend in Hollywood quickly brought down the wrath of the radical right.[21] Congressman Rankin eagerly revived the House Un-American Activities Committee as a permanent House Committee in 1946. "Hollywood is the greatest hotbed of subversive activity in the United States. . . . We're on the trail of the tarantula now," he exalted. He promised to "prove" that the New Deal had pressured the filmmakers into making "the most flagrant Communist propaganda films."[22] Representative Samuel Dickstein fought back. "Were they planning to follow up their previous [1930s] investigation of Hollywood which resulted in the assertion that [famous child actress] Shirley Temple was a Communist?" he asked sarcastically.[23]

HUAC's hearings in Hollywood were conducted in secret. Fourteen witnesses from the right-wing Alliance for the Preservation of American Ideals provided the committee with the names of people they considered subversive. The accused were not informed of the charges against them. HUAC met with studio executives and demanded that they fire everyone on the alliance's list. The producers were defiant, resisting the idea of someone coming in to tell them how to run their studios. They were also aware of Rankin's anti-Semitism. HUAC left in a less than happy mood.

President Truman, who only later criticized the "great wave of hysteria" sweeping over the nation, gave the sputtering witch-hunt a big boost on March 21, 1947, when he issued

Executive Order 9835 ordering a special board of civil service commissioners to search out "disloyal" government employees. The Department of Justice dusted off the old attorney general's list of "subversive" organizations and added hundreds of new groups, including the Committee to End Jim Crow in Baseball, the Chopin Cultural Center, and Nature Friends of America.

Any government employee accused of belonging to or sympathizing with any of the listed organizations could be labeled disloyal and dismissed without a hearing. African Americans and Jews were the two groups most often accused, and many were fired. As a result, government employees began staying away from civil rights meetings for fear of being seen.

By the fall of 1947, Congressman John Parnell Thomas had taken over the reins of HUAC and renewed the Hollywood hearings. Jack Warner, a racetrack buddy of FBI chief J. Edgar Hoover, was the first producer to name names for HUAC. He told his friend director John Huston, "Guess I'm a squealer, huh?" Of forty-three Hollywood luminaries subpoenaed by HUAC, nineteen refused to cooperate. Ten were Jews.[24]

Indictments were handed down against ten of the uncooperative subpoenaed witnesses, six of whom were Jewish.[25] A group of actors, writers, and directors organized the Committee for the First Amendment and sent a delegation to Washington with a petition against HUAC's hearings. Among the committee members were such stars as Humphrey Bogart, Frank Sinatra, Judy Garland, and Gene Kelly. They denounced HUAC as anti-Semitic and condemned its inquiries into people's political beliefs as violating First Amendment guarantees of free speech.

Rankin made no effort to deny the committee's charges. In Congress he rose to read off a list of names on the petition and then went over several slowly, reciting first the signed name and then the birth name: "Danny Kaye . . . and we found out that his real name was David Daniel Kaminsky. . . . June Havoc—We found out . . . that her real name is June Hovick."[26] People gasped as Rankin went down the list, Jew-baiting and Red-baiting the petitioners.

On November 24, 1947, HUAC charged a group of uncooperative witnesses called the "Hollywood Ten" with contempt of Congress. Producers and their lawyers huddled to decide whether those who defied HUAC should be barred from work, or blacklisted. Rabbi Magnin advised the Jewish producers to do just that. He pointed out that in Germany Jewish film producers had opposed Hitler and their industry had been destroyed—"What happened in Germany can happen here."[27] The majority voted to blacklist the accused.[28]

Supporters of the Hollywood Ten approached the American Jewish Committee and asked them to speak out for the indicted men. The committee turned them down on the grounds that the case was a legal matter. Jewish religious leaders lined up on both sides of the issue. Rabbi Benjamin Schultz of Yonkers and others quickly organized the American Jewish League against Communism to prove their loyalty. Rabbi Stephen Wise and the New York Board of Rabbis condemned Schultz for violating the religious law against bearing false witness.

Despite HUAC, the democratic right to speak out was an old habit in the United States that could not be broken in a single stroke. The famous 1954 Supreme Court decision, *Brown* v. *Board of Education*, ordering the desegregation of the nation's public schools, did not start with a group of justices conferring. Along with the NAACP lawyers, many individuals who had never been affiliated with the Left or with civil rights groups exercised their rights to initiate these cases in the late 1940s. One was a young Jewish woman, Esther Brown. The other was Brown's black housekeeper, Mrs. William Swann.[29]

At this time, Brown (not the same Brown as in the court case) lived in South Park, a suburb of Kansas City, Kansas. Mrs. Swann lived there too, but in the segregated black section. While driving Mrs. Swann home one evening, Esther Brown expressed shock at the shack without indoor plumbing that passed as the "separate but equal" school for African American children. A vote for a bond to build a new school in the white part of town was coming up soon, and the two women decided to take action.

A delegation of black parents appeared before the white school board asking for some of the bond money for repairs to their own school. At a parents' meeting, Esther Brown made the same request. "They're not asking for integration—just a fair shake," she said. Her neighbors hooted her down. Later Brown described the audience as "the most gruesome bunch of people I'd ever seen in my life—I mean these were real lynchers." The board offered to give black schoolchildren the used desks from the old white school when the new building for white students was completed.

Esther Brown moved firmly into the integrationist camp. She met with black parents and they discussed legal action. Brown hired an African American attorney, raised money for his fees, and contacted the NAACP in Kansas City. A suit was filed on behalf of several black parents, and students boycotted the black segregated school. Brown worked with the black community to organize private schools in local churches. Nothing could stop her now—not even the firing of her husband or waking up in the night to see a fiery Ku Klux Klan cross on her lawn. The South Park case was won on a technicality, and the new school was ordered to open its doors to all of the children, black and white alike. None of the people involved had any inkling that their small fight in one small corner of Kansas would eventually contribute to the nation's most prolonged and violent social struggle since the Civil War.

By then the presidential election campaign of 1948 was in high gear, and the civil rights issue took the spotlight. Governor Thomas E. Dewey of New York, the Republican candidate, had a good civil rights record. Henry A. Wallace, secretary of agriculture in the Roosevelt administration, became the candidate of the newly formed Progressive Party. He advocated a sweeping civil rights program and criticized Truman's Cold War foreign policy as a danger to world peace.[30] To appease southern Democrats, President Truman stopped talking about civil rights, but the issue of integration of the armed forces wouldn't go away. Military conscription had ended in the fall of 1947, and a new draft law—the Universal Military Training Act—was under consideration.

A. Philip Randolph organized the Committee against Jim Crow in Military Services and Training. Leaders of the group met with Truman and demanded an executive order for military integration. When Truman refused to make a commitment, Randolph publicly announced that his organization would advise all young men, black and white, to refuse to serve in a segregated army. The Baltimore *Afro-American* called Randolph "the John the Baptist of a new Emancipation."[31] Walter White assured Congress that the NAACP disapproved of such militant methods, however, and Congress passed a draft law that maintained segregation.

At the Democratic national convention delegates voted to overturn the official civil rights platform and passed a stronger one. Several southern delegates walked out and formed the States' Rights Party a few weeks later, nominating South Carolina's ardent segregationist governor J. Strom Thurmond for president.

Truman won the Democratic nomination and declared that he would call Congress into special session to give the Republican majority a chance to vote on the liberal civil rights platform promulgated at its convention. With the Thurmond group gone and no one left to offend, the president issued Executive Order 9981, establishing the Committee on Equality of Treatment and Opportunity in the Armed Services. The new committee was instructed to desegregate the armed forces as quickly as feasible. Randolph withdrew his threatened boycott of the draft. The *Nation* proclaimed the "Triumph of civil disobedience."[32]

As Truman had anticipated, at the close of the special session of Congress, nothing had been accomplished. Truman met with black leaders in Harlem and told them to prepare for the "greatest effort in history of the party to attract the black vote."[33] Public opinion polls still showed Dewey in the lead, and Truman knew that the African American vote could mean the difference between defeat and victory for him in key states like New York. W. E. B Du Bois supported the Wallace campaign, as did many others in the civil rights coalition. Democratic Party campaigners launched an all-out Red-baiting campaign against the Progressive Party.[34] William Hastie rushed home from the Virgin Islands to make pro-Truman, anti-Wallace speeches to black audiences. Truman went to Harlem himself,

A. Philip Randolph organized the Committee against Jim Crow in Military Services and Training.

the first president ever to do so, to accept the FDR Memorial Brotherhood Medal.

Truman won an upset victory, receiving 60 percent of the black vote, more than Roosevelt's in 1944. African American voters realized that their votes mattered in presidential elections and hoped that now civil rights would move forward as promised. The NAACP was optimistic, but soon the old pattern was back in place. President Truman appointed some African Americans to federal judgeships and other posts, but there were still no laws against lynching, poll taxes, school segregation, or housing and job discrimination. The *Crisis* angrily commented, "neither the Republicans nor northern Democrats can blame the Dixiecrats."[35]

Yet the streets remained quiet. Potential leaders of a new civil rights movement were silenced by a fierce escalation of the Cold War. In 1948 a Communist government came to power in Czechoslovakia and the Soviet Union blockaded Berlin, preventing U.S. supplies and troops from reaching their portion of Germany's capital. The Western powers organized an airlift, and the blockade failed, but the following year in China Mao Tse-tung led a victorious peasant army into Peking (now Beijing) and proclaimed the establishment of the socialist People's Republic of China.

The Soviet Union tested its first atomic bomb in 1949, setting off a panic in the West. In Canada and Great Britain, several people were charged with being part of a spy ring that had helped the Soviets learn how to make a bomb. In the United States, Julius and Ethel Rosenberg, a left-wing Jewish couple, were arrested and charged with espionage. By then children were being taught to duck under their desks in school for practice air-raid drills.[36]

Only a handful of Americans refused to bend to the atmosphere of fear. They hoped that the witch-hunt for Communists was a tiny blip on the long record of American democracy. But on August 27, 1949, even some of them were were forced to recognize that the Cold War was profoundly changing the thinking of Americans.

On that day, a little over an hour's drive from New York City, near Peekskill, New York, an outdoor concert was scheduled at the Lakeland Acres Picnic Grounds.[37] The event was a fund-raiser for the Civil Rights Congress, established in 1946 to combat racism and anti-Semitism. Paul Robeson, the world-famous African American singer and actor, was to be the featured performer. The local newspaper, the *Peekskill Evening Star*, called on citizens to march in protest against the concert, so the organizers had asked the state police to be on hand to protect them. A few dozen volunteers arrived at the concert site early to set up the stage and folding chairs. At 7:00 p.m, as cars filled with families moved toward the entrance to the Lakeland Acres Picnic Grounds, hundreds of men and women blocked their way and forced them to turn back. Many of the men, wearing veterans' caps, were armed with clubs and blackjacks, and were standing beside a huge mountain of rocks.

Inside the park, the volunteers were attacked by screaming hordes shouting, "Lynch Robeson! Give us Robeson! We're Hitler's boys! We'll finish his job!"[38] The police vanished. The mob set fire to the chairs and bombarded the organizers with rocks. On the hillside a fiery cross burned in the night.

The outnumbered organizers, most of them injured, fought back. Writer Howard Fast described his own harrowing experience:

> *There were thirty-two of us now, with our backs against the truck ... and now into the light come the "new Americans," brandishing the fence rails they have stripped from along the road, swinging their knives and billies.... A Negro lad ... received a rock the size of a baseball full in his face—one moment his face, and then a bleeding mass.*[39]

At ten o'clock the "new Americans" departed as a few state troopers arrived.

Organizers rescheduled the concert for the afternoon of September 4, in the hope that in the glare of daylight fewer goons would dare show their faces. At a support rally in Harlem, dozens of veterans and unionists, both black and white, signed on to act as a defense squad. In Peekskill, banners fluttered in the breeze, emblazoned with the words "Wake up America. Peekskill did!"

A Jewish refugee from Nazi Germany offered his land for the second concert. As the defense squad of 2,500 volunteers guarded the entry roads, more than 25,000 people poured into the area in chartered buses and automobiles. Over a thousand protesters lined the roadside, women and children among them, chanting, "You'll get in but you won't get out." A thousand state and local police left when the defense squad refused to disband.

Paul Robeson arrived at noon. He sang inspirationally, with a sound truck and fifteen veterans and workers, white as well as black, in back of him in case sharpshooters tried to gun him down from the hills behind the stage. At four o'clock, as the 25,000 happy spectators climbed into cars and buses to leave, they found that the three exit roads were blocked by screaming, rock throwing mobs. Windshields and windows of buses were shattered, and glass flew in all·directions. Soon local hospitals and homes were filled with bleeding men, women, and children.

The most severely injured victim was a Jewish New Yorker, Sidney Marcus. His cheekbones and nose were pulverized, and he would remain forever blind in one eye. When Marcus's friends asked a state trooper for directions to the hospital, he told them to find it themselves. As the defense squad left, hundreds of police rushed in and arrested twenty-five of them.

The district attorney of Westchester County blamed the concertgoers, not the mob, for the violence. The American Civil Liberties Union countered, saying that "the Westchester County police permitted the assault."[40] The Ku Klux Klan announced that "Dewey, under high pressure of the Communist Jews 'Outlawed' the Klan in Jew York State, but we are stronger than ever here. . . . Your race KILLED CHRIST on the Cross, we burn it . . . as a warning and a symbol to BEWARE."

The national offices of several veterans' organizations criticized the people who had attacked the concert and caused the Peekskill riot, but did not punish chapters involved in the violence. Eleanor Roosevelt said "This [violence against innocent people] is not the type of thing that we believe in in the United States,"[41] but her voice was drowned out by the rising roar of anti-Red hysteria.

In early 1950, Senator Joseph McCarthy of Wisconsin publicly declared that he had a list of more than two hundred names of Communist Party members working for the State Department. He never produced his list, but he proceeded to hold hearings on supposed Communist subversion of American life. McCarthy's committee soon overshadowed publicity for HUAC.[42] Congress hastily passed the Internal Security Act, overriding Truman's veto. The new law required anyone belonging to the organizations on the attorney general's list to register. People who registered were banned from defense jobs and travel abroad, and few employers dared hire them. Two liberal senators, Hubert Humphrey and Herbert Lehman, amended the act to include the construction of detention centers for accused "subversives" in a national emergency. It wasn't until 1968 that the law was repealed. Many ordinary citizens concerned about building a more just America lost their jobs merely because of a suggestion that they were fellow travelers with Communists. Except for a few court cases, the postwar struggle for equality came to a screeching halt. Old and potential leaders of the civil rights coalition found themselves jobless, hounded, and near desperate.

In May 1950 the military desegregation committee appointed by President Truman reported that the air force, navy, and marine corps had made progress toward integration but that the army had blatantly ignored its recommendations. One month later the Korean War broke out.[43]

Korea had been occupied by Japan for thirty-five years before World War II. After the war the country was divided into two separate nations: North Korea, under Soviet influence; and South Korea, under U.S. influence. The armies of both Koreas were stationed at an invisible dividing line called the Thirty-eighth Parallel. On June 25, 1950, the North Korean army stepped over the line. The United Nations, with the Soviet Union delegate absent, voted to intervene on the side of South Korea. Under the command of General Douglas MacArthur, UN troops, 90 percent of them from the United States, penetrated far into North Korean territory and close to the border of China. On November 26, Chinese troops crossed into Korea and drove the invaders all the way back to the Thirty-eighth Parallel. Armistice talks began in July 1951, but fighting dragged on for two more years. The old boundary was restored—but only after 2 million Koreans and 34,000 Americans were killed.

One advance came out of the bloodshed. During the first year of the conflict, integrated forces proved themselves on the battlefield. Ensign Jesse L. Brown, the first black pilot to fly in naval combat missions, won the Medal of Honor. The all-black Twenty-fourth Infantry was dissolved, and its members were assigned to other units. Social scientists interviewed hundreds of soldiers and concluded that integration had produced positive results.

During the war hysteria surrounding Korea, the Rosenbergs were found guilty and sentenced to death in the electric chair. Many legal authorities believed that the charges against them were trumped up, but every appeal failed. A few sparsely attended rallies were held in defense of the alleged "traitors," with FBI photographers snapping pictures of those who dared to show up. Naturally, most people, especially the foreign-born, were afraid to be seen at such gatherings. In 1952, the McCarran-Walter Immigration Act had permitted the "denaturalizing" of naturalized citizens on political grounds. They could be arrested without a warrant, held without bail, and deported for belonging to one of the attorney general's listed organizations. As the Korean War ended, Ethel and Julius Rosenberg were executed.

In the prevalent Cold War atmosphere, so chilling to free speech, no one was surprised when the Supreme Court refused to review the case of the Hollywood Ten. As they went off to jail, HUAC renewed its hearings into the entertainment industry, this time under a new chairman, Senator John S. Wood of Georgia. Subpoenaed witnesses had no illusions that Wood would be any fairer than John Parnell Thomas had been.[44] Wood, after all, had publicly defended Ku Klux Klan activities as "an old American custom."[45] Subpoenaed witnesses had only a few choices: they could refuse to testify, citing their First Amendment rights, and risk a prison term; they could claim Fifth Amendment privileges against self-incrimination and remain jobless; they could name others as "Reds" and hope to keep on working; or they could leave the country.

Even though some Americans were aware of the ridiculousness of the charges that Hollywood was making Communist films, they kept their silence. Screenwriter Ben Barzman, for example, had written the script for *The Boy with Green Hair*, produced in 1948. It was an almost childlike story of a war orphan persecuted by his schoolmates and their families when his hair turned green—a not very subtle message about prejudice. Barzman and his family left for France before they could be summoned to testify. Some filmmakers wrote their scripts in secret, paying others to submit their manuscripts to producers under false names. The wave of antiracist films stopped dead, and more than forty anti-Communist movies were produced, most of which lost money.

Only a few prominent African Americans were called before HUAC, whose inquisitors were usually satisfied if well-known black athletes, actors, and other performers only bad-mouthed Paul Robeson, who was still a hero of the black community.[46]

The nation's entire cultural scene soon reflected only one ideology—anti-Communism, with a liberal sprinkling of racism and anti-Semitism. Renowned writers like John Steinbeck no longer wrote books on social issues like *The Grapes of Wrath*. Mickey Spillane, whose books sold millions of copies, thrilled his fans with violent anti-Red passages like the following:

> *I killed more people tonight than I have fingers on my hands. I shot them in cold blood and enjoyed every minute of it. . . . They were Commies . . . red sons-of-bitches who should have died long ago.*[47]

Comic books featured similar heroes. America became a cultural wasteland.

The hatred that spewed forth at Peekskill had not been an isolated incident. In July 1951, when an African American couple rented an apartment in all-white Cicero, Illinois, a mob of whites numbering in the thousands battered down a National Guard barricade and set the building on fire. Bombings of synagogues and the homes of civil rights activists were frequent. On Christmas Day 1951, Harry T. Moore, an African American school principal, and his wife were killed when a bomb went off in their Miami home. Their murderers were never found. Walter White said, "The bomb has replaced the lyncher's rope."[48]

In 1950 a lawsuit was brought in the name of Oliver Brown and his daughter Linda against the Topeka, Kansas, Board of Education. The Brown case would lead to the historic Supreme Court ruling against school segregation in *Brown* v. *the Board of Education of Topeka, Kansas*. Jack Greenberg, a Jewish

W. E. B. Du Bois, a founder of the NAACP,
was indicted by the Justice Department
during the McCarthy period.

lawyer, was one of the NAACP assistants to Thurgood Marshall, who argued the case for the NAACP before the Supreme Court.

Civil rights groups were willing to go to the courts but shied away from taking on the witch-hunters. W. E. B. Du Bois had accepted the chairmanship of the Peace Information Center, an organization opposing Cold War policies. In 1951, the eighty-three-year-old founder of the NAACP was indicted by the Justice Department along with other Peace Information Center officers for failing to register as agents of a foreign government. After a nine-month trial, the case was dismissed for insufficient evidence, but in spite of that, the State Department confiscated Du Bois's passport. Throughout his ordeal, the NAACP made no move to support him.[49]

Continued war production inspired by the Cold War kept the economy in high gear. Americans bought homes, appliances, and cars. Many Jewish Americans managed to achieve a decent standard of living, but the vast majority of African Americans continued to live in rat-infested slums, attend second-rate segregated schools, and work at no-future jobs.

Dwight D. Eisenhower was sworn in as president in 1952, but he was reluctant to challenge McCarthyism. Senator Harold Velde of Illinois, a former FBI agent, became HUAC's chairman in 1953. Velde had made his idea of democracy abundantly clear in 1950, when he voted against a bill for mobile library services in rural areas, stating that "Educating Americans through the means of the library service could bring about a change of their political attitude quicker than any other method. The basis of Communism and socialistic influence is education of the people."[50]

Under Velde's direction, HUAC didn't consider any group off limits. It conducted a probe of the clergy in 1953, and then concentrated on the labor movement. Congressman Kit Clardy of Michigan was a supporter of the John Birch Society, probably the most extreme anti-Communist organization in the nation.[51] During hearings in May 1954 in his home district of Flint, Clardy proudly told a story about his college days in 1937, when his friends tossed UAW-CIO organizers into the Red Cedar River. A decorated veteran of World War II who worked in a Flint auto plant wrote to local political leaders asking their help "to stop the violence against me that was instigated by Representative Clardy's hearings." He had been beaten severely several times. When Clardy heard the news, he exclaimed: "This is the best kind of reaction there could have been to our hearings."[52]

Only one or two schools and organizations dared to fight back. In 1954 the Ohio American Legion asked HUAC to investigate Antioch College, sure that the friendly relations between black students and white students at the school were a clear sign of Communist activity. When a teacher refused to testify and was cited for contempt, his colleagues backed him up and the college administration refused to fire him. The indictment was dismissed.

Once in a great while a congressman also dared to criticize Velde and his crowd and was immediately tarnished with the red brush. Representative Elliot Roosevelt, Franklin D. Roosevelt's son, once called HUAC "closer to being dangerous to America in its conception than most of what it investigates." Republican Gordon Scherer of Cincinnati leaped to his feet to insinuate that Roosevelt was under Communist influence.[53]

In the spring of 1954 McCarthy went one step too far when he decided to hold hearings into subversives in the military. Americans tuned in to the televised hearings and watched the senator, who appeared disheveled and, some thought, intoxicated, launch a Red-baiting attack against a young lawyer assisting Joseph Welch, the army's counsel.

Welch rose to his feet in a rage. "Have you no sense of decency, sir?" he demanded, as the spectators in the gallery applauded loudly. Several months later the Senate voted to censure their former hero for "conduct unbecoming a member of the United States Senate." McCarthy was no longer a favorite, but the witch-hunt was alive and well. HUAC's touring-road-show investigations continued for the rest of the decade, which justly earned its nickname "the silent fifties."

At noon on May 17, 1954, the Supreme Court shocked the nation with its unanimous decision in the *Brown* case. The Court struck down the separate-but-equal provision that it had defended since the 1890s.

Asked how long he thought school segregation would continue, NAACP attorney and future Supreme Court justice Thurgood Marshall answered, "Up to five years!"[54] His optimistic prediction was well off target. The decision opened a can of hatred that almost tore the nation apart. But out of the turmoil also came a new black-Jewish alliance—for a while, the strongest and most successful of all.

Chapter seven
"THE CIVIL WAR HAS NEVER ENDED"

It is commonly believed that the violence that swept over the South for more than a decade after the *Brown* decision was the work of fringe terrorist groups such as the Ku Klux Klan and the White Citizens Councils, but that is far from the truth. In many southern states, 80 percent of the voters elected candidates who made continued separation of the races the central focus of their campaigns. Elected state assemblies passed dozens of new Black Codes while mayors and governors called for massive resistance to *Brown*. Law enforcement officers ignored, or even aided and joined, terrorist groups. Armed white racists operated with the unspoken authority of state governments behind them.

The Supreme Court had set no deadline for school integration. In most places African American children continued to attend inferior all-black schools. On May 31, 1955, called "black Monday" throughout the southern states, the Court issued its final decree, ordering integration to be carried out with "all deliberate speed," but still with no target date.[1]

Raging segregationists gathered their supporters. In Mississippi, fourteen men formed the first White Citizens Council. Within the year they had recruited at least half a million members throughout the South. A few brave African American parents filled out applications for their children to attend white schools. They were fired, evicted, and refused credit by businessmen, landlords, and bankers.[2]

Even in the so-called border states, integration was seldom

carried out, even when governors obeyed the law. In Clay, Kentucky, screaming mobs greeted two black children when they attempted to enroll in the grade school nearest their home. When the National Guard escorted them into the school, the white children left.

Initially, African Americans had few allies. But as television camera crews filmed the rising tide of violence against them, thousands of people in living rooms around the country were shocked at what they saw on the evening news. The event that first mesmerized the nation took place at the end of 1955 in Montgomery, the state capital of Alabama. Rosa Parks, the mother of three children and the secretary of the local chapter of the NAACP, worked as a seamstress in a fancy downtown department store where black women could buy clothing but were not allowed to use the dressing rooms. After work on December 1, 1955, Parks climbed aboard a bus for the long ride home, taking the last empty seat in the first row of the "colored" section. A few stops later a white man boarded the full bus and stood in the aisle. The driver ordered Mrs. Parks to give the man her seat, but she decided to stay put. The driver called the police, and Rosa Parks was hauled off to jail.[3] Friends bailed her out, and leading black ministers and activists voted to start a bus boycott. They formed the Montgomery Improvement Association, headed by a twenty-seven-year-old minister named Martin Luther King, Jr.

Beginning on December 5, 1955, and continuing for an entire year, 42,000 of Montgomery's black people walked and car-pooled to their jobs. Close to a hundred leaders of the boycott were indicted for "conspiracy." As lawmen took them off to jail, their mad-dog collaborators, the terrorists, bombed four black churches and fired a shotgun blast through the front door of Dr. King's home. Not only did the boycott continue but another started in Tallahassee, Florida.

A support movement was organized in several northern cities to collect food, clothing, and money for Montgomery. Prominent among the fund-raisers and donors were Jewish Americans.

In late August of 1955, as the boycott entered its ninth

month, a fourteen-year-old black teenager named Emmett Till climbed aboard a train in Chicago for a summer visit to his grandparents in Money, Mississippi, a tiny town deep in the cotton belt of the state, near the Tallahatchie River. Curtis Jones, Emmett's seventeen-year-old cousin, also from Chicago, was to join Emmett in Mississippi. The boys planned to earn some money picking cotton.

Emmett's mother, Mamie Till Bradley, a Chicago teacher, told her son to be careful. Whites had been on a rampage in the Mississippi Delta, determined to keep blacks, who outnumbered them, out of "their" schools and voting booths. Two black voters had been murdered after the Mississippi governor had stated publicly that black people were unfit to vote.[4]

When Emmett arrived in town with his cousin, he made a mistake that cost him his life. He showed some white teenagers a picture of some friends in his graduating class, some of them white. One of the white boys dared Emmett to talk to a white girl inside a store, and after Emmett bought some candy, he waved at the girl and said, "Bye, baby," Chicago style.[5]

A few nights later a knock came at the door. Two armed men ordered the boys' grandfather to turn over "the one who did the talking." Till's grandmother begged them to leave. They struck her on the head with a shotgun. As the kidnappers sped away with Emmett, Curtis called the local police and his mother in Chicago, who immediately called Emmett's mother. Four days later Emmett Till's body was found in the Tallahatchie River, so mutilated that his grandfather had to identify him by the ring on his finger. Emmett's mother demanded the body. "There was no way I could describe what was in that box," she later remembered. "And I just wanted the world to see."[6]

And the world did see. Thousands came to view the body. The nation's leading black publications ran photographs of the battered corpse with one eye poked in. For the first time the white-owned media gave extensive coverage to the murder of an African American in the South.

Medgar Evers, Mississippi field secretary for the NAACP, attended the trial of J. W. Milam and Roy Bryant, the two accused murderers. His presence was duly noted by supporters of the accused. Despite the testimony of Emmett Till's grandfather, Mose Wright, and other eyewitnesses, an all-white jury brought in a verdict of not guilty after only one hour of deliberation. Black witnesses were quickly spirited out of town to "safe houses."

In November, a few weeks after the trial, the Supreme Court outlawed segregation on local bus lines. But the fight was only beginning. Several black ministers met with Bayard Rustin of the Congress of Racial Equality and a Jewish attorney from New York, Stanley Levison, who had been raising funds for southern activists. They formed the Southern Christian Leadership Conference to coordinate activities for nonviolent civil rights groups, and they elected Martin Luther King, Jr., as president.

One of Emmett Till's killers later told southern writer William Bradford Huie that the only reason they had taken Till was because he said he had white girlfriends. "That's what this war's about down here now," he confided.

Southern congressmen agreed, consumed by ridiculous fears that allowing black children and white children to attend school together would lead to intermarriage. On March 12, 1956, they issued a Southern Manifesto, asking the people who had elected them to refuse to obey the Supreme Court's school desegregation order. The phrase "all lawful means" was included in their declaration, but after Till's murderers went free, the terrorists knew they could do even their unlawful work safely.

School integration was simply not happening. Rioters refused to allow even one black student, Autherine Lucy, to attend the tax-supported University of Alabama in 1956.[7] In September 1957, attention was focused on a much publicized integration effort in Little Rock, capital of Arkansas. Daisy Bates, co-owner of a weekly black newspaper and state president of the NAACP, had gathered together a group of black teenage volunteers to seek admission to Central High School. Thirteen students had been selected, but only nine were permitted by their parents to continue as the "chosen ones."[8] Crosses blazed on Daisy Bates' front lawn, but Mrs. Bates refused to bend.

Playing to the crowd on the capitol steps, recently elected Governor Orval Faubus ordered the National Guard to keep the black students out of the school. The plan was for the nine boys and girls to meet at a church and walk to school with ministers, both black and white. Somehow, fifteen-year-old Elizabeth Eckford didn't receive the message and went to the school on her own. A mob of screaming men and women lined the path to the school entrance, cursing and spitting on her as television cameras recorded the scene of hatred. National Guardsmen, pointing their bayonets at the trembling girl, turned her away.

Later Elizabeth Eckford vividly remembered that day:

Somebody started yelling, "Lynch her! Lynch her!" I tried to see a friendly face somewhere in the mob. I looked into the face of an old woman, but she spat on me. I turned back to the guards, but their faces told me I wouldn't get help from them. Then I looked down the block and saw a bench at the bus stop. I thought, "If I can only get there I will be safe."[9]

One white woman shamed the others long enough for Elizabeth to board a bus for home.

The press expressed shock. President Eisenhower, inundated with protest mail and phone calls, federalized the Arkansas National Guard and sent eleven hundred paratroopers to Little Rock. On September 25, with helicopters roaring overhead, the nine black youngsters entered the school with an escort of paratroopers.

In September 1958, three months after the first black student graduated, Governor Faubus ordered all public high schools in Little Rock closed. They remained shut for a year until the Supreme Court ruled the closing unconstitutional and an "evasive scheme to prevent integration."[10] The violence continued for three more years. Mrs. Bates was forced to close down her newspaper, forty-four teachers who supported integration lost their jobs, and the mayor's office was bombed because he had bowed to federal law.[11]

Americans were moved by the plight of children—the battered corpse of Emmett Till and the frightened face of Elizabeth Eckford as she faced the mob. Soon they heard about two other black children, ages only eight and nine.[12] On October 28, 1958, James Hanover Thompson, nine, and David "Fuzzy" Simpson, eight, were grabbed by police and taken to the adult county jail in Monroe, North Carolina. For six days no one knew where they were. Finally their mothers, both low-paid domestics, were notified that their sons would be on trial in half an hour, accused of assaulting three white girls, ages six and seven.

Juvenile Court judge J. Hampton Price acted as judge, lawyer, and prosecutor. Neither the girls nor their parents appeared in court. The judge told the official story: the defendants had climbed into a ditch where the girls were playing and demanded kisses; two of the girls had run away, but the third girl, Sissy Marcus, was forced to kiss Hanover Thompson.

The boys told a different story. They said they were playing with some white boys, and all of them jumped into a ditch where the girls were playing house. David Simpson was busy killing spiders when Sissy recognized Hanover. He had played with her a few years earlier when his mother worked as a maid at her home. Sissy, happy to find him again, kissed Hanover on the cheek. At home, Sissy told her mother the good news: she had found Hanover. Bernice Marcus became hysterical, washed out her daughter's mouth, and called the police.

The judge sentenced the boys to an indeterminate term in reform school. The frantic mothers went to see Robert Williams, president of the Union County NAACP. Together with a black physician, Dr. Albert Perry, Williams was building up the local NAACP branch. But Williams and Perry were frowned upon by the national office of NAACP because they believed in self-defense against white terrorists.[13]

While the NAACP studied Williams' plea for help, he turned to black attorney Conrad Lynn, of New York, known for his willingness to defend unpopular clients. Lynn flew to Monroe and met with Judge Price, raising the violations of the Constitution in what was now known as the Kissing Case. The judge told him to head back north. Instead, Lynn met with the children and their mothers, got the story straight, and called dozens of newspapers. Then he returned to New York and helped set up a defense committee called the Committee to Combat Racial Injustice. Dr. Perry, Lynn, Williams, and the Reverend C. K. Steele of Tallahassee were among several prominent founders, but the longest hours were put in by a Jewish woman named Berta Green, the committee secretary, who helped to obtain international publicity for the Kissing Case victims.

Despite protest rallies in London, Rome, Paris, and Moscow, Hanover and Fuzzy spent Christmas in jail. Finally the NAACP agreed to pay for court appeals. The case had become a tremendous embarrassment to U.S. diplomats abroad. In his own New York county of Rockland, black churches would not allow Conrad Lynn to speak on the case because he wasn't religious, but a Jewish synagogue invited him in. Lynn and Williams persuaded a judge to order a retrial. Lynn urged Attorney General Malcolm Seawell to drop the case and release the children. Seawell's response was carried in many newspapers: "Yes, let them go. Let everything else go too. Our way of life. . . . I say we dare not let these two go . . . Lynn and his ilk . . . want to spit in our faces and rip our sacred traditions to shreds."[14]

Unable to win in southern courts, Lynn reluctantly turned to an old acquaintance, Eleanor Roosevelt. On Lincoln's Birthday he presented Mrs. Roosevelt with a petition signed by 15,000 students at Franklin Delano Roosevelt High School in Rotterdam, Holland, asking for the release of the Kissing Case prisoners. According to Lynn, Eleanor Roosevelt said, "You should have told me before, Conrad. When is this country going to be fair?" and she started to cry.[15] Mrs. Roosevelt called President Eisenhower, who in turn called Governor Luther Hodges of North Carolina. The children were immediately released.

Meanwhile the Southern Christian Leadership Conference (SCLC) grew rapidly. New organizations were born and old ones revitalized. In Atlanta, Georgia, the Student Nonviolent Coordinating Committee (SNCC) was founded to organize student civil rights activities. The older Congress of Racial Equality (CORE) organized in 1942 by a small interracial group of University of Chicago students, believed in nonviolence and had staged lunch-counter sit-ins in the 1940s and early 1950s. In 1957, CORE's training sessions in civil disobedience techniques were suddenly crowded with SNCC members and other new applicants.

On February 1, 1960, in Greensboro, North Carolina, four students from the all-black Agricultural and Technical College sat down at a lunch counter in Woolworth's. Although they were refused service, they occupied the stools until the store closed. People watching the sit-ins on television saw well-dressed young men and women being kicked, burned with cigarettes, and showered with spit. In New York City, some viewers left their couches and set up picket lines at a downtown Woolworth's, carrying signs that read, "We walk so they may sit." Some jumped on buses and headed South to join the new movement. They were arrested and sang the new anthem of the movement, "We Shall Overcome," in their jail cells.

In the next twelve months, more than 50,000 people—most of them black, some white—participated in sit-ins in a hundred southern cities. Over 3,600 were jailed. Merchants were losing business, and not only at their food counters. Many customers, afraid of violence, stayed home. Soon southern businessmen integrated their lunch counters, much to the outrage of White Citizens Council members.

In 1961, CORE organized its first Freedom Rides. Blacks and whites rode buses together through the South, testing a Supreme Court ruling against segregation in bus terminal restaurants and waiting rooms. About two-thirds of the white Freedom Riders were from Jewish backgrounds, but no one talked much about that. Although the demonstrators were upholding the law of the land, the federal government offered them no protection. John F. Kennedy, elected president in 1960, like Truman and Eisenhower before him, was worried about antagonizing white southern Democrats.

In South Carolina, riders were beaten. In Alabama, their bus was set on fire. As they fled the flames, southern police

More than 50,000 people—most of them black, some white—
participated in sit-ins in a hundred southern cities.

stood by. "FBI agents watched, took notes, did nothing."[16]
SNCC activists also took to the road on integrated buses, enduring the "southern hospitality" of terrible beatings in several
cities.

As the word spread, people from all over the nation—not
only students but also ministers, teachers, and housewives—

flocked to join them. James Peck, a civil rights activist since the 1940s, arrived on a Freedom Riders' bus in Birmingham, Alabama, on Mother's Day 1961. He later woke up in the emergency room of a hospital, "beaten almost to death by a Birmingham mob for the 'crime' of trying to eat with a Negro at the Trailways terminal lunchroom."[17] On the Senate floor, Senator Eastland of Mississippi labeled the Freedom Riders "Communists" and singled out Peck, well-known as an anti-Communist pacifist, as an example. But it was not only southern senators like Eastland who Red-baited the Freedom Riders. Former President Harry Truman, later hailed by some historians as an early pioneer of civil rights,[18] called them "meddlesome intruders . . . helping the Communists!"[19]

As the war against segregation in the South heated up, opposition to HUAC also increased.[20] In 1955, Francis Eugene Walter, a northern Democrat, had taken the HUAC helm. He was coauthor of the McCarran-Walter Act of 1952, which was vetoed by Harry Truman and criticized by the Catholic cardinal Richard Cushing.[21] Walter had called Jewish critics of the law "professional Jews" who shed "crocodile tears" over it, and added, "I don't think these people are the kind of people our ancestors were."[22]

But the days of cringing before the power of HUAC were numbered. Several distinguished clergymen fought back.[23] In June 1957 the committee staged televised hearings in San Francisco—for the third time in three years. The suicide of a subpoenaed Stanford research scientist, William K. Sherwood, turned the tide. His suicide note said in part, "I will be in two days assassinated by publicity. . . . I would love to spend the next few years in laboratories, and I would hate to spend them in jail. . . . I have a fierce resentment of being televised."

Walter's response to Sherwood's suicide enraged people. "It certainly is unfortunate that we couldn't interrogate him," he said.[24] Complaining that widespread criticisms of his committee were backed by Communists, Walter next subpoenaed 110 California teachers. This time he was greeted by an avalanche of protest, including a denunciation by Eleanor Roosevelt in her newspaper column of July 12, 1959. A teacher of retarded children had been subpoenaed. Mrs. Roosevelt satirically noted that this "seems a little far-fetched—since it is so difficult to teach retarded children anything, let alone communism."[25]

HUAC suddenly canceled all of the subpoenas[26] when an activist opposition coalition took shape. When HUAC returned to San Francisco in the spring of 1960, more than a thousand people arrived carrying banners of the newly formed Students for Civil Liberties. As the students chanted, "We're still here," and "Abolish the committee," the police rolled out fire hoses. When the students sat down and sang the old union song, "We Shall Not Be Moved," high-powered hoses were turned on them and the police raced through the crowd, swinging their clubs. A few hundred moved to the stairs leading to City Hall.

New York Post correspondent Mel Wax described the bloody scene on the marble staircase:

> *It was down those thirty-eight steps that those who protested the hearing were clubbed, beaten, soaked with high-pressure fire hoses, and dragged kicking and screaming by white-helmeted policemen. I saw it happen. Never, in twenty years as a reporter, have I seen such brutality. San Francisco police hurled women down the staircases, spines bumping on each marble stair. I saw one woman dragged through glass from a broken front-door pane.*[27]

Sixty-four students were arrested, but only one was put on trial. Jewish students had been prominent in the anti-HUAC movement, and some thought it was no accident that the test case focused on a Jewish student, Robert Meisenbach. A year later he was acquitted.

The day after the police assault, about five thousand people rallied and demanded HUAC's abolition. California terrorists reacted exactly like their southern counterparts. In the fall of 1960 they firebombed the office of the Citizens Committee to Protect American Freedom, an anti-HUAC organization based in Los Angeles. Two people were killed in the blast. On January 2, 1961, the House of Representatives voted to dissolve HUAC.

Out in front, American Nazi Party pickets marched in support of the Committee.

In the South, the Civil Rights groups (SCLC, SNCC, and CORE) pushed voter registration campaigns. In Albany, Georgia, over a thousand people went to jail for attempting to register during 1961–1962. Eight years after the *Brown* decision, segregation remained in effect in most southern public schools and universities, maintained by a terror campaign.[28]

One lone black man, James Meredith, an air force veteran, obtained a federal court order for admission to the University of Mississippi. Meredith was escorted onto the campus by U.S. Marshals as television newsmen filmed the historic moment. Mississippi's governor, Ross Barnett, stood waiting at the administration building, saying for the benefit of television audiences that he would go to jail before he would allow Meredith to walk through the hallowed halls of "Ole Miss." Fierce rioting broke out on campus and in the nearby town of Oxford, as 2,500 students and adults, waving Confederate flags, threw gas bombs and bricks at the federal marshals and reporters for fifteen hours. President Kennedy ordered in 12,000 troops. When the rioting ended, four hundred people had been injured and two were dead. A French journalist wrote: "The Civil War has never ended."[29]

The riots had been filmed, and the faces of those who had committed murder could have been identified from the footage, but no arrests were made. James Meredith attended class escorted by three hundred soldiers.

With school integration at a virtual standstill, voter registration became a top priority. African Americans had been denied the vote through registration tests based on obscure clauses in state constitutions that most college graduates would have failed. SNCC decided to focus on the South's industrial hub—Birmingham, Alabama.

Martin Luther King, Jr., went north to raise bail money, recruit lawyers, and help train volunteers. On April 3, 1963, as crowds of Easter season shoppers filled Birmingham's downtown stores, activists sat down at department store lunch counters, and pickets tried to persuade black shoppers to go home.

James Meredith (left), the African American who integrated the University of Mississippi, and Jack Greenberg (right), NAACP legal counsel. Man in the center is not identified.

The police arrived in force. As hundreds of demonstrators were shoved into paddy wagons, others took their places.

Police commissioner Eugene "Bull" Conner, an ardent segregationist, decided to get tough. On May 3, when hundreds left the Reverend Fred Shuttlesworth's Sixteenth Street Baptist Church, police and firemen were waiting for them. When they marched downtown singing, tear gas filled the area and high-pressure hoses were turned on them. Then a new tactic was tested: Trained police dogs attacked, biting, snarling, and going for throats. Again, millions watched the true-life horror show on television, and some packed up and headed for Birmingham.

On May 7, some 2,500 demonstrators marched. The next day there were more than 3,000. At least a thousand were jammed into Bull Connor's jails. A stream of water hit the Reverend Fred Shuttlesworth in the chest and slammed him against a building. An ambulance took him to a hospital. "The whole world is watching," the demonstrators chanted.

They were right, and the White House was watching too. Protests poured in from all over the world. President Kennedy sent a representative to attempt to negotiate a resolution to the conflict. Birmingham business establishments had lost large amounts of money during the disturbances. They decided to permit the integration of lunch counters and open a few jobs to blacks.

The mayor called them traitors, and the terrorists went to work. Bombs exploded at a few homes and at the motel where Martin Luther King, Jr., and other movement people were staying. In the black section of town, riots broke out. Many young people had already lost confidence in nonviolent tactics. They grew even angrier in April when William Moore—a white CORE member dedicated to nonviolence who had announced that he would make a solitary freedom walk through the South wearing a sign that read "Equal rights for all"—was found dead at the side of a road, the victim of a sniper's bullet. Then, in June, Medgar Evers too was killed—shot in the back in the driveway of his home in Jackson, Mississippi.

A. Philip Randolph proposed a mass summer demonstration in Washington, D.C., just as he had done more than twenty years earlier. On August 28, 1963, a quarter of a million Americans streamed into the capital to join the March on Washington for Jobs and Freedom. They marched together to the Lincoln Memorial, where they heard Dr. King's stirring "I have a dream" speech.

Eighteen days later, four little black girls attending Sunday school in the basement of Birmingham's Sixteenth Street Church were blown to pieces when a bomb exploded. "We give love—and we get this!" a young boy screamed.[30]

On November 22, 1963, President John F. Kennedy was assassinated in Dallas, Texas, and Lyndon B. Johnson was inaugurated. Civil rights leaders decided to concentrate next on violence-prone Mississippi.[31] They announced a massive voter registration drive during Freedom Summer 1964. SNCC organizers put out a call for volunteers, and the response was enormous. By early summer a virtual army of 1,200 young people arrived.

Many writers have commented that Jewish youth made up one-half to two-thirds of the volunteers. Jewish Americans like Esther Brown had been prominent in the struggle for school desegregation both before and after the *Brown* decision. After *Brown*, the New York chapter of the American Jewish Congress filed the first brief against school segregation in the North, in Englewood, New Jersey.

In truth, the black-white alliance for civil rights in the 1960s was often a black-Jewish alliance. Stanley Levison, a Jewish lawyer, was one of Martin Luther King's most trusted advisers. The records of the various civil rights organizations show that Jews donated between half and three-quarters of the money collected. At CORE, two Jewish men, first Marvin Rich and later Alan Garter, were fund-raisers and speechwriters. Half of the white lawyers who defended protesters in the South were Jewish.

Although most researchers agree on the surprising number of Jews, they differ on the explanation. For a few like Henry Schwartzchild, a Freedom Rider and onetime official of the Anti-Defamation League, there was "a line that ran through

Auschwitz to Birmingham." Schwartzchild, a refugee from Nazi Germany, "resolved he would never be a 'good German,' standing by in the face of evil."[32]

However, most Jewish participants in the Freedom Summer Project were young. They certainly had heard about Auschwitz, but it is not likely to have been the main reason for their decision. One young volunteer, Michael "Mickey" Schwerner, for example, had lost several relatives at Auschwitz. His mother had questioned his decision to buy a German-made Volkswagen in 1957 when he turned eighteen. But Schwerner believed that young Germans were not like their Nazi-influenced parents. He wanted to buy a Volkswagen to show his confidence that there could never be another Auschwitz.[33] He would go to Mississippi sure that racists could change.

Author Irving Howe argues strongly against the most common explanation for Jewish involvement in civil rights struggles—the notion of self-interest, racism being a cousin to anti-Semitism. Howe notes that "blacks had served . . . as a kind of buffer for American Jews. So long as native hatreds were taken out primarily on blacks, they were less likely to be taken out on Jews." Self-interest dictated enjoying the benefits of the buffer, but "the majority felt themselves to be allies of the blacks . . . at times just about the only reliable allies the blacks had."[34]

A few writers point to the social justice aspects of the Jewish religion as the reason for Jews defending civil rights. But most of the activists were not religious. Although they were proud of their cultural backgrounds, they knew little about Judaic law.

Professor Arthur Liebman offers an explanation that emphasizes family influence.[35] Many of the activist Jewish youth were raised by parents who had been involved in the social struggles of the 1930s. In early childhood they were taught to oppose racism, support unions and social legislation, and most of all, care about less fortunate people.

Both Michael Schwerner and Andrew Goodman fit this Jewish family profile. Goodman was very young when a family friend who was about to go to jail for defying the McCarthy committee, visited on his birthday. Andrew started to cry, his

Mickey Schwerner

mother later told journalist Jonathan Kaufman. "Why does he have to go to jail on his birthday?" he asked.[36] Kaufman claims that Jewish youth from radical homes "often made the strongest impression on blacks in the South. They stayed the longest and became more fully involved in the struggle than students visiting for a summer or fund-raisers dashing off a check."[37]

Whatever their reasons, several Jewish youth had already decided by the spring of 1964 to spend their summer vacation

Andrew Goodman

in Mississippi. They did not know that forty-three-year-old Sam Bowers, imperial wizard of the White Knights of the Mississippi Klan, believed that Jews were the instigators of the trouble made by "good Negroes" of his state. According to journalist Jack Nelson, "Bowers sometimes wore swastikas on his arm. On occasion, he was known to click his heels in front of his old dog and throw stiff Nazi salutes, exclaiming, 'Heil Hitler!'"[38]

Twenty-four-year-old Michael Schwerner headed south with

his wife, Rita, in his second Volkswagen on January 15, 1964. Still believing in basic human decency, he "found another Auschwitz before he reached his twenty-fifth birthday."[39] Schwerner had been working at a settlement house on New York's Lower East Side. He and Rita were both CORE activists, deeply affected by the terrible events in Birmingham. The young couple had agreed to work in the South for at least a year. On January 16, they arrived in Jackson and were assigned to establish a community center in the small Mississippi town of Meridian.

By the end of February, the center was in full swing, holding story hours for children and evening classes for adults. African American history was taught to many who knew nothing about Crispus Attucks or Dorie Miller. There were heated discussions of violence versus nonviolence. Black stars like Sidney Poitier and Harry Belafonte came down to entertain.

One of Michael and Rita Schwerner's first recruits was a young black man named James Earl Chaney—J.E. to his friends. Chaney was born to a poor Meridian family in 1943. He had his first contact with the civil rights movement and his first real trouble when he attended Harris Junior College and made friends with the sons of the president of the Mississippi NAACP. When the three boys wore NAACP buttons to school, they were suspended. After a second conflict with the principal, J.E. was expelled. He drifted into the Meridian community center. By the time summer rolled around, he and Schwerner were working together to start a Freedom School with members of a black church in the town of Longdale, Mississippi.

At Queens College in New York City in April, Andrew Goodman, age twenty, listened to Aaron Henry, a Mississippi black man, encourage the audience to sign up for Freedom Summer. Andy had joined the picket lines in front of Woolworth's and other support demonstrations, but all of them had been in the safety of the North. He had thought about joining a Peace Corp-type project in Mexico, but Henry made Mississippi sound far more important.

The Schwerners and Chaney met Goodman at a nonviolence training session in Oxford, Ohio. On June 20, 1964, as

James Chaney

the four of them drove toward Meridian, the U.S. Senate passed the Civil Rights Act, forbidding discrimination in public accommodations, employment, and educational facilities receiving federal funds. The mere rumor of the possibility of such a law had stimulated yet more violence. In May, two black men, twenty-year-old civil rights activist Charles Eddie Moore and his nineteen-year-old friend James Dee, both of Meadville, Mississippi, never came home after an afternoon of river fishing.

Weeks later, fishermen found their bodies. Charles Marcus Edwards confessed to the FBI that he and James Ford Seale had tied the young men to trees, beaten them unconscious, and then thrown them in the river. The two murderers were never brought to trial by Mississippi prosecutors.[40]

When the Schwerners, Chaney, and Goodman reached Meridian, they heard that the Longdale church had been burned down. The next day the three young men headed to Longdale to check out the situation. Goodman had been in Mississippi for only one day, but he wanted instant experience. The trio never returned. Police in nearby Philadelphia, Mississippi, said they had taken them to jail for speeding and then released them. President Johnson sent in two hundred FBI agents to investigate. Politicians announced that the whole thing was a hoax perpetrated by civil rights leaders.

On August 4, 1964, the bodies of Chaney, Goodman, and Schwerner were found buried deep in an earthen dam after paid informers passed the information on to the FBI. The three had been executed by a firing squad.

The story gradually unfolded, ugly bit by ugly bit. The killing of Schwerner had been planned for months. Mississippi's terrorists had decided to exterminate the "Jew-boy with the beard at Meridian" as soon as they could get him to their turf outside of Lauderdale County. Chaney and Goodman had been killed simply because they were there.[41]

Schwerner's wife, Rita, and his parents wanted him buried beside his friend Chaney, but there was no way to bury blacks and whites near one another in Mississippi, as one writer expressed it "unless you bury them at night in a dam."[42] In Meridian, whites jeered as seven hundred people marched to the church for a memorial for James Earl Chaney. His mother, Fannie Lee Chaney, told mourners:

When my child drove nights out here to this church, who grudged him so much that they thought they had to kill him? Mickey Schwerner, he was just like a son of mine. James told me: "Mama, that man's got sense. He's down here to help us. I'm not gonna let him do it by

hisself.... I'm gonna stand up by his side." That was my
child, as well as Mickey and Andy. And I just don't want
those children's work to be in vain.

David Dennis, CORE field secretary in Mississippi, gave anything but a nonviolent speech when he wept and told the
mourners, "I've got vengeance in my heart tonight."[43]

Michael Schwerner's body was cremated. Andrew Goodman was buried in a Jewish cemetery in Brooklyn. Mrs. Chaney
flew to New York for the service. One mourner said, "The
question today is not whether Andrew Goodman is dead—the
question is whether we are dead."[44] The parents of the three
slain civil rights workers linked arms as television cameras
recorded the sad proceedings.

In 1967 seven men were finally given light prison sen-
tences of from three to ten years for taking the lives of Chaney,
Goodman, and Schwerner. Twelve other men were released.
Author William Bradford Huie ends his account of the events
of the summer of 1964 by commenting, "Two governors, Paul
B. Johnson, Jr., and George Wallace, contributed to this murder.
They entertained, comforted, and encouraged the same peo-
ple who later 'activated Plan Four' [extermination] against 'the
Jew-boy with the beard at Meridian.'" After the belated trial,
Huie approached one of the murderers and recorded the fol-
lowing dialogue:

> *"Well, you were correct on one point. You killed*
> *Schwerner because you said he was an 'agitatin, trou-*
> *ble-making, nigger-loving, Communist, atheistic Jew out-*
> *sider.' It's true that he called himself an atheist."*
> *"He did, huh? He didn't believe in nothing?"*
> *"Oh yes" I said, "he believed in something. He*
> *believed devoutly."*
> *"What'd he believe in?"*
> *"He believed in you."*
> *"In me! What the hell!"*
> *"Yeah," I said. "He believed in you. He believed love*
> *could conquer hate. He believed love could change even*

you. He didn't think you were hopeless. That's what got him killed."[45]

By then many movement people were beginning to wonder whether nonviolence and love could change the twisted brains of the racists. About 200,000 southern Jews, less than a quarter of 1 percent of the South's population, were sharply aware that anti-Semitism played a major role in terrorist attacks against movement workers. They knew that the reference to Schwerner as "the Jew boy with the beard" was no accident. In 1957, a few dozen clergymen, including rabbis, had issued the "Atlanta Manifesto" calling for compliance with the *Brown* decision. After their statement, several synagogues and Jewish community centers had been dynamited. A small group of southern Jews supported the civil rights movement, but the vast majority kept quiet.

Rabbi Perry Nussbaum, of Temple Beth Israel in Jackson, Mississippi, had come there from Pittsfield, Massachusetts, in 1954, the year of the *Brown* decision. His predecessor had stayed away from controversial issues and most of the 140 Jewish families in the city were equally cautious. In the early 1960s, Nussbaum helped organize a biracial committee collecting money to help rebuild bombed or burned-out black churches. His name was placed on Bowers' hit list, but well below Schwerner's name.

After the tragic Freedom Summer of 1964, at the University of California at Berkeley a few students set up tables with SNCC literature. Campus officials ordered them to take the tables down. College, they were told, was for education not agitation. Jack Weinberg, a Jewish community activist and former student, made a rousing speech on campus. A police car arrived and Weinberg was arrested. A thirty-two-hour sit-in prevented the patrol car from leaving the campus. The free speech movement (FSM) was born. On December 2, 1964, students occupied the Berkeley administration building. Police roughly expelled them.

Soon college students throughout the nation began organizing to win free speech, civil rights, and an end to the escalating, unpopular war in Vietnam. Berkeley students held shop-ins at the city's supermarkets, leaving filled wagons at the checkout counters until they won the hiring of black work-ers.[46] According to Professor Liebman, the Berkeley students "set the pattern for Jewish involvement in New Left actions on [other] campuses. The majority of FSM [free speech move-ment] leadership was Jewish."[47]

In the South, the Civil Rights movement focused next on Selma, Alabama, where Sheriff Jim Clark, a Bull Connor clone, presided over "peacekeeping." In January 1965, Clark arrested 280 people who were trying to register to vote. Martin Luther King, back from a trip to Europe, where he had received the Nobel Peace Prize, joined them in the Selma jail. Outside the courthouse, supporters were pushed back with nightsticks and electrified cattle prods and then thrown into jail too. On February 18, James Lee Jackson, a local civil rights leader, was fatally shot. About five hundred people, with Hosea Johnson of SCLC and John Lewis of SNCC in the front row, started a protest march across the Pettus Bridge. They were met with a barrage of swinging billy clubs, tear gas, and bullwhips. John Lewis collapsed to the ground in front of television cameras. That night all of America watched police poke Lewis's still form and club the fleeing marchers.

With Lewis in a hospital bed, his skull fractured, Dr. King returned from a fund-raising trip and announced a new march in Selma. Thousands of people headed for Selma, not only stu-dents but religious leaders, congressmen, trade union leaders, and celebrities. In the front line, Rabbi Abraham Joshua Heschel locked arms with Dr. King and, with him, led the march across the Pettus Bridge toward Montgomery. Twenty-five thousand strong they marched down the highway carry-ing flags and singing "We Shall Overcome." When they reached the capital, Governor Wallace refused to meet with them, but no one dared attack 25,000 people. Instead, far from the view of television cameras, a carload of Klansmen murdered Viola Gregg Liuzzo, a white housewife from Detroit, as she and a young black SCLC volunteer drove marchers back to Selma. One of the klansman was an FBI informant.[48]

Four months later the Voting Rights Act of 1965 declared

voter registration tests illegal. Five days after that, a shocking-
ly destructive riot broke out in Watts, Los Angeles's black ghetto. Many Jewish-owned stores were looted and burned. After
visiting the devastation of the riot area, Dr. King told Bayard
Rustin, "I worked to get these people the right to eat ham-
burgers, and now I've got to . . . help them get the money to
buy it."[49]

In 1966 more than ten thousand blacks in Selma registered
and voted Jim Clark out of office, but the terrorists did not give
up so easily. In Grenada, Mississippi, after four thousand voters
registered, men with ax handles and chains assaulted black children as they left an elementary school.[50] The days of the nonviolent movement were numbered and the Black Power
movement was being born. SNCC announced its opposition to
the war in Vietnam and the draft. By then many SNCC members
were carrying guns to defend themselves. To many of them, voting rights had not accomplished much. SNCC's communica-
tions director, Julian Bond, was elected to the Georgia
legislature but was refused a seat. In 1966, Stokely Carmichael
was elected SNCC chairman. Unlike John Lewis, a southerner,
Carmichael had been raised in New York City and had attended the prestigious Bronx High School of Science, where he had
made many Jewish friends. His first visit to the South had been
as a Freedom Rider.

It can be said that June 1966 marked the unofficial end of
nonviolence in the civil rights movement. It came, oddly
enough, when James Meredith, the lone integrator of Ole Miss
and a symbol of nonviolence, announced that he intended to
walk from Memphis, Tennessee, to Jackson, Mississippi, alone
and unarmed, in a "march against fear." On the second day of
his walk, three bullets hit him. Amazingly, he survived.

SNCC took up Meredith's march, only this time they did not
sing "We Shall Overcome" or shout out slogans of love and
brotherhood. Instead, they chanted "We want Black Power."
The meaning of the slogan was explained to the press: SNCC
leaders were tired of telling people not to defend themselves.
Like Robert Williams in North Carolina and the Deacons for
Defense in Louisiana, they intended to fight back.

In the next weeks and months it also was very clear that

the young black leaders intended to run their own show. At that stage there was no hint of anti-Semitism in the remarks of leaders like Carmichael. When he discussed the future role of whites, he said,

> *One of the most disturbing things about almost all white supporters has been that they are reluctant to go into their own communities—which is where racism exists—and work to get rid of it. . . . They often admonish black people to be nonviolent. They should preach nonviolence in the white community. Where possible, they might also educate other white people to the need for Black Power. . . . The organizational role is next. . . . It is our position that black organizations should be black-led and essentially black staffed, with policy being made by black people.*[51]

Bayard Rustin, who had worked with white CORE volunteers for decades, told a story that reinforced Carmichael's position:

> *A Negro girl down south is working in a SNCC headquarters where she had been told about "participatory democracy." Get this scene—I saw this myself. The girl is struggling to prepare a mimeographed press release which has to be out by three o'clock. She can't type or spell. A white girl comes in, looks at it in horror, says, "Move Over" and knocks it off in three minutes. That happens over and over.*[52]

Both Rustin and Carmichael were talking about whites, in general, not specifically about Jews. CORE endorsed the Black Power concept, but the NAACP quickly disassociated itself from it. Author Irving Howe described the situation this way:

> *As black nationalism grew stronger . . . the black revolution expelled whites from its ranks. Very often that meant Jews. . . . The achievement of autonomy meant that there would have to be some irksome jostling of*

friends, and in general, despite bruised feelings, Jews
active in the cause came to understand this.What they
could not tolerate was the fringe of blacks who pushed
a legitimate need to be on their own into a repetition
of coarse anti-Semitic slogans.[53]

But at that time very few blacks voiced "coarse anti-Semitic slogans." By then most Jewish activists were deeply involved in an organization called Students for a Democratic Society (SDS) and in the growing antiwar movement. Several of them supported the Black Power cause. By the latter half of the sixties, SDS had close to 100,000 members nationally, most of them on college campuses.The ideology of SDS, often called the New Left, was a peculiar mixture of antiracist, humanitarian, and antiestablishment ideas, with some of the socialist humanism of the Old Left added to the brew. Professor Liebman estimated that a "significant proportion of leaders and activists within the SDS were Jewish."[54] He also noted that 90 percent of Jewish college students claimed that they participated in the student antiwar strikes that swept the nation's campuses in May 1970.

In 1966, SNCC launched a "Black is Beautiful" campaign to help young African Americans develop a better self-image after years of living in a racist culture. Huey P. Newton and Bobby Seale founded the Black Panther Party for Self-Defense in Oakland, California, in 1966. The Watts riot had proved to Newton that economic injustice was at the root of the problems of African Americans.Within a year or so, the Panthers had over two thousand members in forty chapters nationwide, organizing breakfast programs and classes for poor black children.

The issue of black anti-Semitism in the 1960s was not raised on any significant scale by confrontations between Panthers or SNCC members and Jewish activists. The trouble started instead in the quiet New York City suburb of Mount Vernon when a school integration dispute made headlines.[55] African Americans made up 30 percent of Mount Vernon's population; 45 percent were Italian; and only 15 percent were Jewish. Many of the whites, including the Jewish president of Mount

Vernon Parents and Taxpayers, opposed the local black community's integration plan.

Knowledgeable African Americans realized that there were liberal Jews and conservative Jews and learned to differentiate between the two. But American racism had taught too many people for too long to label whole groups. An incident in Mount Vernon started a process rolling where some Jews saw *all* blacks as anti-Semitic, and some blacks saw *all* Jews as racists. During a heated argument at a school board meeting, Clifford A. Brown, a thirty-two-year-old CORE official, rose to his feet and said, "Hitler made a mistake when he didn't kill enough of you."

Black leaders everywhere criticized Brown's shocking remark, but James Farmer of CORE stopped short of demanding Brown's resignation, saying that he wanted time to study the "context" of the remark. Will Maslow, the executive director of the American Jewish Congress and a member of CORE's national leadership body, resigned from CORE, asking, "Can you conceive of any context that would make Mr. Brown's outrageous statement permissible? Can you conceive of any situation that would justify the kind of tirade that calls for more acts of genocide?"[56] No one seems to have raised the most important point: that neither Clifford Brown nor those Jews opposed to integration represented the thinking of *all* blacks or *all* Jews.

Farmer issued a stronger statement, but by then several Jewish members of CORE's National Advisory Committee had resigned and contributions had dropped precipitously. The Mount Vernon incident created a serious rift in the remaining black-Jewish alliance, but not yet a divorce.

In the summer of 1966, Martin Luther King, Jr., launched an effort to open up Chicago's de facto segregated housing and schools. When he led a march for housing integration in Marquette Park on Chicago's exclusively white southwest side, he was deeply shocked by the welcoming committee he faced:

A thousand whites surrounded the six hundred marchers, waved Confederate flags and Nazi banners, chanted "Nigger go home!" and let loose a fusillade of

*rocks, bottles, and bricks. One brick struck King on the
head and knocked him to the ground. "I've never seen
anything like it," King said. "I've been in many demonstrations all across the South, but I can say that I have
never seen ... mobs as hostile and hate-filled as I've seen
in Chicago."*[57]

Over the next weeks, King negotiated a compromise settlement
with Chicago's politicians. Local SNCC leaders considered the
agreement a sellout and criticized King in public. Responded
King: "Whenever Pharaoh wanted to keep the slaves in slavery,
he kept them fighting among themselves."[58]

King became even more concerned about black life in
urban America when uprisings swept through the ghettos of
several large cities in 1967. In Detroit, a large area was burned
to the ground. President Johnson's National Advisory
Committee on Urban Disorders, known as the Kerner
Commission, "blamed white racism" and "pervasive discrimination and segregation in employment, education and housing" for the riots.[59]

Shortly after the Kerner Commission report, Congress
passed the Civil Rights Act of 1968, expanding the government's role in protecting civil rights. President Johnson stepped
up his War on Poverty, setting up poverty agencies in ghetto
areas to create neighborhood job-training and other programs.
But with the war in Vietnam consuming billions of dollars,
there just wasn't enough money to do the job.

African Americans had marched in antiwar demonstrations
as individuals, but on April 15, 1967, wearing signs that read
"No Vietnamese ever called me nigger," a huge Harlem group
swept down Fifth Avenue to join a larger antiwar demonstration in Central Park. On that day there were no ugly confrontations between blacks and Jews. Anti-Semitic and racist
remarks came only from white prowar onlookers.[60]

In June 1967, Israel defeated its Arab neighbors in the Six
Day War and occupied a large chunk of Arab lands. Although
most of the antiwar Jewish youth were not members of Zionist
organizations, they recoiled when speakers at a Black Power

conference in Newark referred to the American system of justice as a "racist Zionist legal system."[61] Jewish liberal organizations reacted with great fury when SNCC published articles denouncing Zionism and charging Israelis with atrocities against Arabs. A Black Panther publication was even more virulent.[62]

Black leaders like Bayard Rustin and Martin Luther King took issue with these attacks, but "Increasingly, many Jews and many whites believed it was people like Carmichael who spoke for black America."[63] Some Jews opposed Israel's policies but were still offended by the anti-Semitism displayed by a few African American leaders who blamed all Jews for Israel's actions as well as the problems of America's blacks. Journalist Kaufman noted that "Jews were a part of the liberal coalition that had promised so much. Blacks were angry and frustrated, and they struck out, hitting those closest to them, the Jews."[64] Several prominent Jews who had continued to support the civil rights movement despite the Black Power emphasis now resigned from CORE.

Southern terrorists knew or cared little about divisions between blacks and Jews. As far as they were concerned, Jews had been the guiding lights behind the Voting Rights Act. Sam Bowers, awaiting trial for the murder of Chaney, Goodman, and Schwerner, hatched a plan to terrorize Rabbi Nussbaum.[65] After dark on September 18, 1967, a bomb rocked Jackson's Beth Israel temple. Fortunately, Nussbaum and his family were safe at home.

An FBI informant inside the Klan had a tape recording of Klansmen proposing to bomb the temple while it was full of worshipers. When one Klan member objected to the killing of children, the leader said: "To hell with that. Little Jew bastards grow up to be big Jew devils"[66]—almost the same words used by Laura Delano in response to the proposal that 20,000 Jewish refugee children be permitted to enter the United States.

Violence was becoming the hallmark of the 1960s, just as conformity had marked the 1950s. Malcolm X, who had marshaled a growing following among ghetto blacks, had been murdered in 1965, apparently by Black Muslim opponents.

Martin Luther King, Jr. was gunned down three years later. Dr. King's long-delayed announcement in early 1968 of his opposition to the war in Vietnam and his new emphasis on economic justice had made him more than ever "a chief target of the FBI. . . . As a Senate report on the FBI said in 1976, 'the FBI tried to destroy Dr. Martin Luther King.'"[67] A sniper's bullet felled King on April 4, 1968, when he was in Memphis, Tennessee, lending his support to striking black sanitation workers.

The response to King's murder was far from nonviolent. Rioting raged in dozens of cities. Thirty-five out of thirty-nine of the people killed were black. Then, on June 5, 1968, Robert Kennedy, brother of the assassinated president, met the same fate as he campaigned for the Democratic Party presidential nomination.

Three weeks later, on June 29, Rabbi Nussbaum and his wife, Irene, were awakened by a huge explosion—their house had been bombed. The Nussbaums ran out of their house. Irene Nussbaum was weeping. The Reverend Douglas Hudgins, pastor of Jackson's First Baptist Church, arrived and expressed his sorrow to the Nussbaums with NBC taping the scene. Perry Nussbaum was in no mood for condolences. Later that night television audiences heard his angry remarks to Hudgins:

> *If you had spoken out from your pulpit after the synagogue was bombed and told your people it was wrong to have done that, this wouldn't have happened. . . . I don't want to hear how sorry you are! . . . It's the Sunday school lessons from the New Testament in Baptist churches that lead people to commit such terrible acts.*

In the North, black-Jewish relations worsened as school issues deepened the fissures. In the mid-1960s, the Ford Foundation had established grants for an experiment to begin in 1968 in three New York City school districts—the I.S. 201 Complex in Harlem, Ocean Hill-Brownsville in Brooklyn, and Schwerner's old settlement house district, the Two Bridges area of lower Manhattan. African American and Puerto Rican parents were given some community control over the schools in these demonstration districts in order to play a more prominent role in the education of their children. Antiracist white students and teachers, most of them Jewish, enthusiastically supported the project.

For a brief time it looked as though the old Harlem alliance for the schools would be reborn, but the situation had changed enormously since then. Albert Shanker, president of the United Federation of Teachers (UFT), was a far cry from the teachers Harlem parents had loved in the 1930s, like Alice Citron. Shanker had joined the march from Selma to Montgomery in 1965, but Black Power was not his cup of tea. As head of a pow-erful union he, like many other white liberals, supported inte-gration but flinched at the idea of parents and community leaders running *his* schools. One of the first actions by black principals in the three demonstration districts was to send year-end transfer notices to teachers considered racist by the major-ity of parents. Shanker, defending his union members, called a strike, and in the fall most teachers walked out. Some of the schools remained open, staffed by pro–community control UFT teachers, many of them Jewish.

The New York school situation swiftly deteriorated. Seventy percent of the teachers asked to remain by the new community-based school boards were white, and half of them Jewish; nevertheless, the issue of authority remained. The UFT didn't want its power undermined. Charges of anti-Semitism and racism flew back and forth, and the media rushed in to cover the conflict.

Individual remarks by African Americans and Jews were handled as though they were the opinions of thousands. Little coverage was given to the white and Jewish teachers who had stayed at their posts. Every nasty turn of events was made into a major crisis. For example, at a speakout in Greenwich Village, one black person said that Goodman and Schwerner had head-ed South to "assuage their consciences," causing further charges and countercharges throughout the city.[68] Community control was radically watered down, and the black-Jewish alliance underwent a vindictive divorce—during a period of white backlash against black civil rights gains, when the alliance was most needed.

On December 4, 1969, before dawn, a squad of heavily armed Chicago police raided an apartment where a few Black Panthers lived and fired dozens of rounds of ammunition at the sleeping occupants. Two young leaders, Fred Hampton and Mark Clark, were killed in their beds. Later it became known that the raid was all part of a massive FBI program of counter-intelligence known as COINTELPRO that went on between 1956 and 1971, taking almost three hundred actions against just about all black groups.[69]

In May 1970, in the wake of a U.S. invasion of Vietnam's neighbor, Cambodia, the National Guard opened fire on protesting students at Ohio's Kent State College. Four unarmed students, three of them Jewish, were killed; nine were wounded. Ten days later, police attacked black students at Jackson State College in Mississippi, killing two and wounding twelve. At several schools black students and white students joined briefly together in mutual opposition to the war and to official violence at home. Their nationwide strike shut down campuses throughout the nation. But by then it was clear that the black-Jewish alliance, hammered together for decades, had been severely crippled.

Chapter

BRIDGE BURNING VERSUS BRIDGE BUILDING

Many people who had been deeply involved in the movements of the 1960s wondered if much had really changed. Sam Bowers served six years in federal prison for his role in the slaying of the three civil rights workers and then walked the streets free. Rabbi Perry Nussbaum never fully recovered from Bowers' terror campaign. He retired in 1973 and moved to San Diego, where he died on March 30, 1987, the same year that an armed chapter of the White Knights of the Ku Klux Klan was established in Kansas City, Missouri. Calling themselves "fanatical ecologists," they asserted, "We want to give our Aryan children a future with a land with fresh air, unpolluted water and soil."[1]

On the other hand, the witch-hunt of the 1950s was discredited by almost everyone as a disgraceful blotch on American history. Those who had turned over names to the witch-hunters in the 1950s were left with few friends.[2] As author Victor Navasky said,

> *They named names because they thought nobody would remember, but it turned out to be the one thing that nobody can forget.... Now society at large began to see them the way their victims saw them—not as heroes but as villains, not as patriots but as betrayers. The stigmatizers became the stigmatized....The denouncers rather than the denounced were stuck with their new identity.*[3]

A few Jewish institutions on the Lower East Side in New York City survived, but their clientele had changed. The Educational Alliance now served neighborhood blacks and Puerto Ricans, as well as some aged Jewish women who still lived in the area.[4] The Hebrew Sheltering and Immigrant Aid Society helped settle new generations of Russian Jewish refugees fleeing a rising tide of Soviet anti-Semitism since the 1970s. Their numbers skyrocketed in the 1990s when they found it easier to leave their homelands after the collapse of Soviet communism. A few of the old immigrant Jewish garment union leaders were slowly replaced by young college-educated Jewish negotiators with little or no experience in the trade, and by a sprinkling of black and Puerto Rican garment workers. When the NAACP accused the unions of excluding minorities from leadership posts, they were told that few of the new workers were interested in the union.

Because of civil rights legislation, a more prominent black middle class emerged—politicians, educators, lawyers, actors, athletes, and a handful of businessmen and other professionals. Some became quite well known. Black models and actors appeared on television, stage, and screen, and several black filmmakers, like Spike Lee, achieved fame. This caused many white Americans to believe that blacks were making it, and that remedial programs like affirmative action were superfluous.

This type of thinking, together with the onset after 1973 of economic hard times that led to massive layoffs of previously secure workers, fueled a white backlash against African Americans. The rise of the Radical Right and the presidencies of Ronald Reagan and George Bush reversed many earlier civil rights gains. Several Supreme Court decisions, by narrow 5-4 votes, legalized the resegregation of the nation's schools and undermined affirmative action in the job market. Said former U.S. Civil Rights Commission director Arthur Fleming, "There has been an across-the-board breakdown in the machinery that six previous administrations constructed to protect civil rights."[5] During the first two years of the Clinton administration, some of the lost ground was regained, but the decline of the economy continued to play havoc with minorities.

More than a few commentators began to compare the situation to the events right after the post-Civil War Reconstruction period. Unfortunately, by the mid-1990s, the much celebrated black middle class included only a fraction of black America. The economic downturn starting in the mid-1970s and the so-called Reagan Revolution deregulating the economy helped to concentrate income and power in the hands of a fortunate few at the expense of the vast majority—especially blacks. A 1994 joint report by the Commerce Department and the Department of Labor noted that society was becoming polarized into one of "haves and have-nots." It declared that the ongoing wage gap "between white and nonwhite workers" was very likely to spell an end to social stability and democracy.[6]

Until the early 1970s, more than a quarter of Jewish Americans were earning their living as professionals and semi-professionals, as compared with 14 percent of the rest of the population; but very few Jews were employed "in the great banks, insurance companies, public utilities, railroads, and corporation head offices . . . and in the Wall Street law firms."[7] As the recession continued, the situation for Jews worsened, too.

Little known was the fact that more than a few Jewish people lived in poverty. Elderly retired workers surviving on small pensions or Social Security payments continued to live in ILGU cooperative housing built in the 1930s, in Lower East Side tenements, and in ramshackle sections of Coney Island and Brighton Beach, Brooklyn. Recent immigrants trying to make a fresh start in a downturned economy were their neighbors. In Crown Heights and Williamsburg, Brooklyn, at least 25,000 ultra-Orthodox Jews, the Hasidim, who had fled the Nazis in the 1940s, lived in neighborhoods adjoining black ghettos.[8]

Today up to two-fifths of full-time employed Americans earn less than the unrealistically low poverty level set by the government for a family of four. The 1990 census categorized one-tenth of whites as poor, compared with 31.9 percent of African Americans and 28.1 percent of Latinos. Half of America's black children live in poverty, and African Americans continue to experience the highest unemployment rates. Blacks also represent a disproportionately large share of the nation's 7 million homeless. At the same time, nearly half of all Americans live in suburbs, but 95 percent of them are white.[9]

As stated by the nation's only independent congressman, Vermont's Bernard Sanders, a socially conscious Jew,

The richest 1 percent of our population now owns 37 percent of the wealth, more than the bottom 90 percent of the people.... Economic decisions that wreck the lives of millions of American families are made by a handful of CEOs [chief executive officers].... Our wages, health care, vacation time, parental leave and educational opportunity lag behind much of the industrialized world.... One in every ten American families now puts food on the table only with the aid of food stamps.[10]

By the mid-1990s, the alliance between African and Jewish Americans seemed to have totally unraveled. Incidents like Brooklyn's 1991 Crown Heights riots, after the traffic death of a black youngster and the stabbing of a Hasidic youth, pitting blacks against Hasidic Jews, did not help matters. The Nation of Islam's widespread distribution of its anti-Semitic tract *The Secret Relationship between Blacks and Jews* and the hate-mongering speeches of its representatives at schools and on national television further damaged the fading alliance.

When the NAACP's director, the Reverend Benjamin Chavis, Jr., invited Nation of Islam leader Louis Farrakhan to a national black leadership conference in the spring of 1994, the debate escalated. Chavis had called anti-Semitism "a hideous form of racial hatred and bigotry."[11] But he had the difficult job of reinvigorating the NAACP, which had gone into a long membership decline after the 1960s. Court cases were no longer the major issue of the day, and Chavis had started to talk about economic justice in his public calls for uplifting what he called the "black underclass." Farrakhan's Nation of Islam had attracted many poor African Americans and jailed blacks. Since the NAACP invited just about all black organizations to become members, Chavis did not exclude Farrahkan.

Other Muslim groups worried that people would believe that their religion preached hatred. At a Denver mosque, Imam Abdullah, the head of the Mountain States Islamic Association, an organization made up largely of blacks who have converted to traditional Islam, clasped hands with a local rabbi as an audience of Jews and Muslims approvingly applauded.[12]

Henry Louis Gates, Jr., professor of English and chairman of the Afro-American studies department at Harvard, offered an explanation for black attacks on Jews:

The strategy of these apostles of hate, I believe, is best understood as ethnic isolationism—they know that the more isolated black America becomes, the greater their power. And what's the most efficient way to begin to sever black America from its Allies? Bash the Jews, these demagogues apparently calculate, and you're halfway there.[13]

A Brooklyn College historian wrote a letter to *The New York Times* blaming the Cold War era for preventing the development of a new generation of more responsible black leadership. He wrote:

As 1948 dawned, black leaders in the United States included the old socialist W. E. B. Du Bois, still playing a leadership role in the NAACP; the left wing artist and activist Paul Robeson; and Ben Davis, a card-carrying Communist from Harlem who had been reelected to the New York City Council in 1945 by a large margin.

... by 1958, Du Bois had been ousted from the NAACP for failing to go along with the cold war consensus, Robeson had been persecuted and isolated for similar reasons, Davis had only recently emerged from prison after violation of the Smith Act. Part of the cost of the cold war ... is the undermining of an indigenous left-wing African American leadership. Once this happened, the stage was set for the rise of various forms of narrow nationalism. ... When Malcolm X repudiated

narrow nationalism and turned toward a more inclu-
sive version of Islam and more direct political engage-
ment, he was murdered.[14]

While today's headlines more than ever feature animosity
between minority groups, especially blacks and Jews, a number of new multiracial organizations have sprung up around
the country in an attempt to heal old wounds and renew the
struggle for social and economic justice. They are beginning to
teach a few people from all groups about the alliances and victories of the past.

In Chicago, Harold D. Washington, an African American
reform Democrat, twice was elected mayor against the old
Democratic Party machine. He succeeded by putting together
a multiracial, multiethnic "rainbow coalition."

New school reform movements have popped up throughout the nation, including one that Mayor Washington encouraged in the 1980s. It was based on the 1960s notion of
community control, but with a new twist.

This time the community control advocates relied on multiracial alliances, realizing they had a better chance of winning
that way. They sought also to lend momentum to the new multiculturalism curricula being mandated by several leading state
educational authorities from California to New York. According
to Mayor Washington's planning commissioner, Chicago's multicultural community control movement "overturned the city's
best established bureaucracy in the name of educating children."[15] Supported by many minorities and the volunteer assis-
tance of several college math and science teachers, the
community control movement drew the support of many different groups, including local business executives. It turned
Chicago's ghetto schools over to enthusiastic parent-teacher
councils. The children's advocacy group Design for Change
helped promote the change and has spread its work to other
school districts.

College campuses, too, despite the much publicized scenes
of ugly racism, have shown some signs of reviving the socially
conscious alliances of earlier times. A loose coalition of many

different groups supported the South Africans' long struggle against apartheid, successfully putting pressure on U.S. corporations to withdraw investments from a South Africa ruled by an undemocratic white racist minority regime. African Americans, Jews, Latinos, and Asians often worked side by side in these and similar struggles, such as the one to end U.S. intervention in Central America in the 1980s. Many veterans of the 1960s social movements pitched in too, giving rise to hope for an alliance between old and young, as well.

In a few places, new groups were born, which were reminiscent of the human rights organizations that sprang up after the post-World War II racist violence. African Americans and Jewish Americans were largely responsible for organizing the National Coalition Building Institute, headquartered in Washington, D.C. In Albany, New York, Jewish American Lawrence Rosenbaum and African American Rodney Little co-founded Bridge Builders, stressing person-to-person contact. Bridge Builders ran a special program for elementary school children in 1994, funded and hosted by SUNY Albary, including sessions where two storytellers narrated the same story, one from the black and one from the Jewish perspective.[16]

Despite the consumerist "me first" culture of the 1980s and 1990s, many of the children of socially conscious Jews and African Americans remained attached to the caring traditions of their grandparents. Eli Smith, a third-generation Jewish American, wrote the following poem when he was eleven, paying homage to his father's sense of social justice.

Phil Glickman:The Nightly Call [17]

"Hello, Mike? Phil."
Every night at dinner
He slept
in the back of a caddie
a friend at a garage let him.
Though he was homeless my father found him a home
and now he'll call every night to discuss the theories of
Einstein with my father.
None of which dad understands.

Though he is a self taught man
he excels in
philosophy, advanced math
and other subjects I only begin to comprehend.
He was an old seafarer
land locked
in a
big city.
But with friends
for a compasss
he has found
his way home.

It could only be hoped that a new generation of black and Jewish youth would once again build bridges to close the gap between all oppressed peoples.

SOURCE NOTES

INTRODUCTION

1. University of Chicago Sociology Department study, reported by ABC News, Apr. 15, 1994.

2. *Nightline*, May 16, 1994.

3. Quotes are from *The New York Times*, Jan. 26 and Feb. 23, 1994.

4. *New York Times*, Apr. 16, 1994, p. 9. For more on these disputes, see Chapter 8.

5. *Time* magazine, Feb. 7, 1994, p. 37.

6. For a thorough explanation of multiculturalism, see James D. Cockcroft, *Latinos in the Struggle for Equal Education* (New York: Franklin Watts, 1995), Chapter 8.

7. Quoted in Jonathan Kaufman, *Broken Alliance* (New York: New American Library, 1988), p. 50.

8. Quoted in Gabrielle Simon Edgcomb, *From Swastika to Jim Crow: Refugee Scholars at Black Colleges* (Malabar, Fla.: Krieger, 1993), p. 25.

9. Quoted in Arnold Adoff, ed., *Black on Black: Commentaries by Negro Americans* (New York: Macmillan, 1968), p. 182.

10. Quoted from Dr. King's column, *Baltimore Afro-American*, March 3, 1966.

11. Quoted in Howard Zinn, *A People's History of the United States* (New York: Harper Perennial, 1980), p. 23.

CHAPTER ONE

1. For an extremely moving portrayal of Columbus's discovery and its consequences, see Howard Zinn, *A People's History of the United States* (New York: Harper Perennial, 1980), pp. 1–22.

2. For an excellent description of African civilizations and the early slave trade, see Langston Hughes and Milton Meltzer, *African American History* (New York: Scholastic, 1990), especially pp. 5–34.

3. Quoted in Dorothy Sterling, *Tear Down the Walls! A History of the American Civil Rights Movement* (Garden City, N.Y.: Doubleday, 1968), p. 21.

4. Quotes are from Sterling, pp. 23 and 24.

5. For more on the background of the Jews, see Roberta Strauss Feuerlicht, *The Fate of the Jews* (New York: Times Books, 1983), pp. 32–57.

6. The Jews actually spoke Ladino, an ancient form of Spanish still existing today.

7. From *Humanities News*, Sept. 1991.

8. In *Humanities News*, Sept. 1991, an article appeared raising the issue of motivation. The author concluded that the monarchs expelled the Jews and Muslims and allowed the torment and destruction of the Indians of the Caribbean because they were "determined to unite their kingdom under one religion or law." The robbing of the Spanish Jews and the subsequent plunder of the Americas seem to contradict this theory.

9. This story is adapted from Kenneth Libo and Irving Howe, *We Lived There Too* (New York: St. Martin's-Marek, 1984), pp. 39-48.

10. One of the Sephardim, David Ferrera, earned his living peddling goods in the area. When a customer refused to pay him, he took his merchandise back. He was then arrested and kept in prison until he paid a stiff fine and apologized for his bad manners!

11. The persecution had come suddenly. A century earlier in Poland Jews had enjoyed even more privileges than the Sephardim had under Muslim rule. Their luck ran out in 1648. The huge estates of absentee Polish Catholic landlords had been farmed by starving Ukrainian Orthodox serfs, who were allowed to keep only a tiny portion of their crops. The landlords had hired a few Jews to collect taxes and crops from the serfs. In 1648 the serfs rebelled. Over 100,000 Jews were murdered, and their neighborhoods were burned to the ground by mobs of Ukrainians and Poles. See Feuerlicht, pp. 53-54 for more details.

12. In 1737, for example, in a hotly contested local election for the New York Assembly, a Puritan lawyer declared that Jews should not have been permitted to vote. At the time, there were about three hundred Jews in the city. The assembly immediately voted to ban Jews from voting, an order that remained in effect until after the Revolution. In Pennsylvania, Jews were allowed to vote but were barred from holding public office until 1790. In Roger Williams' Rhode Island colony, where another group of Sephardim had arrived, Jews were barred from voting and from public office despite the fact that Williams went down in history as a man who believed in religious tolerance.

13. Libo and Howe, p. 59. Feuerlicht, pp. 44-45.

14. Quoted in Robert G. Weisbord and Arthur Stein, *Bittersweet Encounter* (Westport, Conn.: Negro Universities Press, 1970), p. 23.

15. In Newport, Rhode Island, Rivera and Lopez, two Sephardic merchants, sent ships to the West African coast in the 1760s, as did Isaac Eliezer and Samuel Moses. For more details see Weisbord and Stein, p. 23, and Libo and Howe, p. 61.

16. The lives of America's slaves have been recounted in literally hundreds of volumes. Recommended highly is Zinn, Chapter 10, pp. 167-205, and Sterling, pp. 33-42.

17. In Virginia, a slave code of 1705 permitted dismemberment. In 1723 Maryland, blacks could have their ears severed if they hit a white person.

18. For further details about indentured servitude see Zinn, pp. 42-47.

19. See Zinn, p. 49, for details.

20. In a local election in New York in the 1730s, campaign literature asked voters to join "'Shuttle' the weaver, 'Plane' the joiner, 'Drive' the carter, 'Snip' the tailor, 'Smallrent' the fair-minded landlord, and 'John Poor' the tenant" to get rid of those in office who were "People of Exalted Stations" who scorned "those they call the Vulgar, the Mob, the herd of Mechanicks." Quoted in Zinn, p. 51.

21. In North Carolina, a so-called Regulator movement existed from 1766 to 1771. It was supported by most of the taxable population of about 8,000. Its purpose was to prevent high taxation and foreclosures on the property of small farmers as well as to protect the rights of squatters and tenant farmers. When a few reforms passed by the North Carolina Assembly did not end the movement, the militia moved in. Six men were publicly hanged.

22. For further details on these land wars, see Zinn, pp. 62-65.

23. Quoted in Zinn, p. 51.

24. On October 2, 1750, an advertisement in the *Boston Gazette* had listed Attucks by name: "Ran away from his Master William Brown of Framingham...a Molatto [sic] Fellow, about 27 years of Age, named Crispas, 6 feet two inches high." The original advertisement is duplicated in Robert W. Mullen, *Blacks in America's Wars* (New York, Monad Press, 1973), p. 10.

25. See Zinn, p. 58.

26. Quoted in Zinn, p. 76.

27. Quoted in Zinn, p. 62.

28. Quoted in Sterling, p. 32.

29. Quoted in Zinn, p. 75.

30. For details of rebellions, see Zinn, pp. 70-81.

31. For details on Jewish participation in the American Revolution, see Libo, pp. 74-77, and J. George Fredman and Louis A. Falk, *Jews in American Wars* (Washington, D.C.: Jewish War Veterans of America, 1954), pp. 6-19.

32. For details on black Revolutionary heroes, see Mullen, pp. 11-14; Hughes and Meltzer, pp. 73-75; and Lou Potter, *Liberators* (New York: Harcourt Brace Jovanovich, 1992), pp. 4-5.

33. New York allowed drafted white men to send free blacks in their stead and also offered freedom to all slaves who served. Massachusetts and Rhode Island allowed slaves to replace their masters in the battlefields. They were key to the victory at Saratoga, New York. During the terrible winter of 1778, about four hundred black soldiers froze at Valley Forge with George Washington. In June, seven hundred took part in the Battle of Monmouth Courthouse. James Robinson, a slave, was awarded a gold medal for conspicuous bravery under fire at the final battle of the War for Independence at Yorktown on September 19, 1781.

34. Quoted in Mullen, p. 133.

35. These military men did not criticize the performance of black men

but only the idea of armed Africans. Brigadier General William Heath informed Samuel Adams that he was "never pleased to see them mixing with white men." Potter, p. 6.

36. Quoted in Zinn, p. 179.

CHAPTER TWO

1. As land-hungry southern planters and western farmers eyed the vast lands of Mexico's Texas, debate over extending slavery to the new areas centered on that issue rather than on the morality of the war. For details on the Mexican War and its impact on Mexicans in the Southwest, Texas, and California, see James Cockcroft, *The Hispanic Struggle for Social Justice* (New York: Franklin Watts, 1994); Hedda Garza, *Latinas: Hispanic Women in the United States* (New York: Franklin Watts, 1994); and Howard Zinn, *A People's History of the United States* (New York: Harper Perennial, 1980), pp. 147–66.

2. Zinn's book remains one of the best sources on life in the early United States. On the early struggles of workers, see pp. 207–46; on slavery, pp. 167–205.

3. For further details on the struggle to abolish slavery, see Dorothy Sterling, *Tear Down the Walls! A History of the American Civil Rights Movement* (Garden City, N.Y.: Doubleday, 1968), and Langston Hughes and Milton Meltzer, *African American History* (New York: Scholastic, 1990).

4. The Militia Act of 1792 included only male citizens between the ages of eighteen and forty-five. In 1798, Secretary of War Henry Knox officially named the excluded groups (Hughes and Meltzer, pp. 73–76).

5. Quoted in Robert W. Mullen, *Blacks in America's Wars* (New York: Monad Press, 1973), p. 16.

6. Quoted in Sterling, p. 59.

7. Quoted in Hughes and Meltzer, p. 97.

8. For more details on this case, and for the story of the health of slaves and the role of African American doctors and nurses, see Hedda Garza, *Women in Medicine* (New York: Franklin Watts, 1994).

9. Middle-class reformers, most of whom were white women, organized on a broad range of issues, from shortening the work hours of women workers in the textile mills to improving the conditions in orphanages, poorhouses, institutions for the mentally ill, and prisons. See Zinn, pp. 114–15, and Garza, *Women in Medicine*.

10. This story is told by Sterling, p. 46.

11. Quoted in Sterling, p. 60.

12. Quoted in Sterling, p. 64.

13. Quoted in Bertram Wallace Korn, *American Jewry and the Civil War* (Philadelphia: Jewish Publication Society of America, 1951), p. 15.

14. The most thorough study of anti-Semitism in American literature is Sol Liptzin, *The Jew in American Literature* (New York: Block, 1966).

15. Ralph Waldo Emerson, America's best known philosopher and

essayist, wrote against anti-Semitism in his journals. The New England poets Henry Wadsworth Longfellow, John Greenleaf Whittier, and Oliver Wendell Holmes all attempted to present a fairer image of the Jews. Many men who were elected to the early legislatures worked hard to remove special laws restricting Jews from political participation.

16. For details, see Libo and Howe, pp. 95–97, 98.

17. Quoted in J. George Fredman and Louis A. Falk, *Jews in American Wars* (Washington, D.C.: Jewish War Veterans of America, 1954), p. 26.

18. One of the Strauss brothers, a family of Bavarian Jews who settled in Georgia, ran a general store. Later two of the sons became the owners of Macy's department store in New York City. Oscar Strauss, who later served as secretary of commerce and labor under Theodore Roosevelt, had this to say about his boyhood in Georgia: "I never questioned the rights or wrongs of slavery....The grown people of the South, whatever they thought about it, would not, except in rare instances, speak against it, and even then in the most private and guarded manner. To do otherwise would subject one to social ostracism....quoted in Libo and Howe, p. 141.

19. Quoted in Weisbord and Stein, pp. 24–25.

20. Weisbord and Stein, p. 30.

21. For more details, see Fredman and Falk, pp. 39–53.

22. For details, see Fredman and Falk, pp. 53–55.

23. Quoted in Korn, p. 123.

24. For the full story of African American participation in the Civil War, see Joyce Hansen, *Between Two Fires* (New York: Franklin Watts, 1993).

25. On Thanksgiving Day 1865 Rabbi Bernhard Felsenthal of Chicago delivered a sermon on the end of slavery, saying in part: "and now they will be free.... And should the nation not rejoice? Still many more millions of white people languished in slavery. They were fettered by the shackles of prejudices.... And was not the name *abolitionist* a name of disgrace? And now this name has become a name of honor.... The white people have become emancipated just as well as the black people. The abolitionists were the true statesmen of the nation." Quoted in Korn, p. 23.

26. For details, see Sterling, pp. 69–93.

27. For details on Klan activities during this period, see Sterling, pp. 82–89.

28. For the story of America's Latinos, see Cockcroft, *The Hispanic Struggle for Social Justice*; Cockcroft, *Latinos in the Making of the United States* (New York: Franklin Watts, 1995); and Garza, *Latinas*.

29. Thomas Bell's *Out of this Furnace* is an autobiographical novel about several generations of Eastern Europeans working in the steel mills of Pennsylvania.

30. For the full story of African Americans at the end of the nineteenth and in the first decades of the twentieth century, see Paul Jacobs and Saul Landau with Eve Pell, *To Serve the Devil* (New York: Vintage Books, 1971), pp. 109–25; Hughes and Meltzer, pp. 175–87; Robert L. Harris, Jr., *Teaching*

African American History, rev. ed. (Washington, D.C.: American Historical Association, 1992), pp. 35-42; Hasia R. Diner, *In the Almost Promised Land: American Jews and Blacks, 1915-1935,* (Westport, Conn.: Greenwood Press, 1977); Lenora E. Berson, *The Negroes and the Jews* (New York: Random House, 1971); and Jack Salzman, ed., *Bridges and Boundaries: African-Americans and American Jews* (New York: Braziller, 1992).

CHAPTER THREE

1. For the full story of the Statue of Liberty, see John Higham, *Send These to Me: Immigrants in Urban America,* rev. ed. (Baltimore: Johns Hopkins University Press, 1984), pp. 71-80; and Anne Novotny, *Strangers at the Door* (New York: Bantam Books, 1974), p. 96.

2. For details of this history, see Novotny, pp. 79-111.

3. These passages on the Russian Jewish immigrants are based on several sources including Charlotte Baum, Paula Hyman, and Sonya Michel, *The Jewish Woman in America* (New York: Dial Press, 1976), especially Chapters, 2, 3, and 4; Higham, pp. 81-147; Abraham J. Karp, *Haven and Home: A History of Jews in America* (New York: Schocken Books, 1985), pp. 170-246; Roberta Strauss Feuerlicht, *The Fate of the Jews* (New York: Times Books, 1983), pp. 68-110; Irving Howe, *World of Our Fathers* (New York: Harcourt Brace Jovanovich, 1976); and Hasia R. Diner, *In the Almost Promised Land: American Jews and Blacks, 1915-1935* (Westport, Conn.: Greenwood Press, 1977), pp. 3-13.

4. Quoted in Feurlicht, p. 55.

5. The power behind Czar Alexander II was Konstantin Pobedonostsev. He devised a three-part solution to the Jewish "problem": one-third of the Jews would be killed during pogroms; one-third would convert; and the remaining third would be "encouraged" to leave.

6. Quoted in Karp, p. 111.

7. For more on the changes in the ethnic and racial composition of Harlem, see Gerald Meyer, *Vito Marcantonio* (Albany: State University of New York Press, 1989), pp. 4-5; Karp, p. 41.

8. Others spread out to other cities where jobs existed. In 1900 the Jewish population of Chicago was 285,000; Baltimore, 50,000; Philadelphia, 150,000; Detroit 25,000; Boston 60,000; Cleveland, 60,000; and St. Louis, 40,000.

9. Quoted in Robert G. Weisbord and Arthur Stein, *Bittersweet Encounter: The Afro-American and the American Jew* (Westport, Conn.: Negro Universities Press, 1970), p. 7.

10. A complete study of the relationship between German Jews and Eastern European Jews is in Ande Manners, *Poor Cousins* (New York: Coward, McCann & Geoghegan, 1972). See especially pp. 84-90 and 107-114.

11. In the 1890s, for example, department store owner Nathan Strauss built his own hotel in Lakewood, New Jersey. Exclusive hotels rapidly sold

out, and the area became a segregated Jewish vacation retreat. See Higham, pp. 127-130.

12. The Industrial Removal Office set up by well-off German Jews in 1900 managed to relocate 40,000 Jewish immigrants. For details, see Kenneth Libo and Irving Howe, *We Lived There Too* (New York: St. Martin's-Marek, 1984), pp. 282-95, and Karp, pp. 179-81.

13. The United Jewish Charities of Rochester, New York, for example, made the point clearly, calling the newcomers "a bane to the country and a curse to all Jews. The Jews have earned an enviable reputation in the United States, but this has been undermined by the influx of thousands who are not ripe for the enjoyment of liberty and equal rights, and all who mean well for the Jewish name should prevent them as much as possible from coming here" (quoted in Karp, p. 116).

14. Quoted in Karp, p. 160. But his words were lost in a tornado of criticism.

15. For details on the settlement house movement, the Educational Alliance, and the Educational League, see Manners, pp. 133-138, and Sherry Gorelick, *City College and the Jewish Poor* (New Brunswick, N.J.: Rutgers University Press, 1981), pp. 28-32.

16. About this "Jewish hunger for education" myth, Gorelick says that "if the U.S. institutional structure had remained as it was when the Eastern European Jews arrived, the Jewish 'Passion for education' might have remained an unrequited love.... See p. 6.

17. The Hanus Report. See Howe, *World of Our Fathers*, p. 275.

18. Quoted in Gorelick, p. 122.

19. Quoted in Karp, pp. 155-156. Areas with houses of prostitution were called red-light districts.

20. For the history of socialist organizations in the United States, see Arthur Liebman, *Jews and the Left* (New York: Wiley, 1979), especially pp. 38-69.

21. See Howe, *World of Our Fathers*, pp. 287-324. Rabbi J. Silverman of Temple Emanuel, a congregation composed largely of German Jewish businessmen and their families, first called his "poor cousins," the Eastern European Jews, "naturally repulsive and repugnant to the refined American sensibilities." He then expressed his more tangible fear about workers "forced to join labor unions, against their own inclinations" and the "Socialist who delights in creating dissension" (quoted in Gorelick, p. 29).

22. Quoted in Karp, p. 105.

23. Quoted in Baum, Hyman, and Michel, p. 152. A biography of Schneiderman and the full story of the Triangle fire appear in Baum, Hyman, and Michel, pp. 148-61.

24. For more on the Frank lynching, see Lenora E. Berson, *The Negroes and the Jews* (New York: Random House, 1971), pp. 29-33; Diner, pp. 14-15.

25. For the full story of African Americans at the end of the nineteenth century and in the first decades of the twentieth century, see Paul Jacobs and

Saul Landau with Eve Pell, *To Serve the Devil* (New York: Vintage Books, 1971), pp. 109-25; Langston Hughes and Milton Meltzer, *African American History* (New York: Scholastic, 1990), pp. 175-87; Robert L. Harris, Jr., *Teaching African American History*, rev. ed. (Washington, D.C.: American Historical Association, 1992), pp. 35-42; Diner, pp. 16-19.

26. Benjamin Tillman, a white farmer living in poverty since the Civil War became the leader of the new Farmers Alliance in 1886. The party called for lower taxes, fairness to small farmers, and educational opportunity for their children, the same aspirations that concerned black southerners. Unity between the two racial groups might have led to reforms, but instead the Populists helped to increase the racist atmosphere and gained little for themselves. Tillman was elected governor, then senator, and served in the Senate until his death in 1912. See Berson, pp. 27-28.

27. The National Baptist Convention had 3 million members in 1895. The National Association of Colored Women formed in 1896, with the stated purpose of "improvement" of the race. See Harris, p. 32.

28. One of the first national labor organizations, the Knights of Labor, eventually organized 60,000 black workers. But in 1886, when the American Federation of Labor came to the fore, white-only policies were the rule in most of its member groups.

29. The largest black college was Howard University in Washington, D.C., established with Freedmen's Bureau funds. With the end of Reconstruction, funding disappeared. Most of the other black colleges were smaller and poorer than Howard, and many closed their doors in the early years of the twentieth century, unable to meet new educational standards. For more on this severe blow to black higher education, see Hedda Garza, *Women in Medicine* (New York: Franklin Watts, 1994), especially Chapter 6.

30. The history of these three groups, and the differences between them, are covered by Harris, pp. 35-41; Berson, pp. 62-95.

31. Harriot Hunt, one of the first women doctors in the United States, applied to simply attend lectures at Harvard in the 1840s. Three black men, including Martin Delaney, had made the same request and had been granted permission to audit all lectures. Students rioted, stating that the "socially repulsive" blacks would lower the prestige of their diplomas. The college administration agreed to student demands, and Hunt also was barred. For details on Harvard's long record of racism and sexism, see Garza, Chapter 3.

32. Quoted in Berson, p. 71.

33. Quoted in Harris, p. 36. For more on the life and work of W. E. B. Du Bois, see Patricia and Frederick McKissack, *W. E. B. Du Bois* (New York: Franklin Watts, 1990).

34. When a white woman accused a black man of rape—though she later retracted the charge—white gangs raced into black neighborhoods attacking every black in sight and burning down homes and businesses. Two black men were lynched—an elderly barber and an 84-year-old shoemaker;

neither was accused of anything. The shoemaker's only "crime" was that he had been married to a white woman for three decades. Thousands of black families fled from Springfield. Some walked to St. Louis and Chicago when nearby towns blocked their entry. See Berson, pp. 86–87.

35. In retrospect, many historians have agreed that the labels "accommodationist" for Washington and "integrationist" for Du Bois are far too simplistic. Booker T. Washington had been raised among barely literate people and saw an urgent need to provide them with survival skills. W.E.B., the educated son of free northern blacks, believed that black people had been deprived of their own culture under slavery and had to develop a culture of their own. He wanted full equality for African Americans but never urged them to accept white culture as their own. He could be called an early multiculturist who believed that the integrationist melting-pot idea could only mean that black people would attempt to become dark-skinned whites, part of one homogeneous culture.

36. See John Hope Franklin, *From Slavery to Freedom* (New York: Knopf, 1967), p. 472.

37. In Chicago in 1915, the first black man was elected to the city council.

38. Quoted in David Levering Lewis, "Parallels and Divergences: Assimilationist Strategies of Afro-American and Jewish Elites from 1910 to the Early 1930s," in Jack Salzman, ed., *Bridges and Boundaries* (New York: Braziller, 1992), p 22. See also Berson, p. 59.

39. Among them were Edison's *Cohen's Advertising Scheme* (1904) and Griffith's *Old Isaacs, the Pawnbroker* (1907). See Sarah Blacher Cohen, *From Hester Street to Hollywood* (Bloomington: Indiana University Press, 1983), pp. 259–60.

40. For the full history of African Americans in early films, see Thomas Cripps, *Slow Fade to Black: The Negro in American Film, 1900–1942* (New York: Oxford University Press, 1977). See also Berson, pp. 88–89.

41. A few minor concessions were granted. Since there were no training facilities for black officers, Dr. Joel E. Spingarn, the Jewish chairman of the executive committee of the NAACP, persuaded the army to set up one such camp. The Wilson administration also appointed a powerless black adviser to the secretary of war—Booker T. Washington's former confidential secretary, Emmett J. Scott. For the story of black participation in World War I, see Lou Potter, *Liberators: Fighting on Two Fronts in World War II* (New York: Harcourt Brace Jovanovich, 1992), pp. 20–29.

42. See Hughes and Meltzer, pp. 197–98.

43. For details, see Liebman, pp. 421–26.

44. For details, see J. George Fredman and Louis A. Falk, *Jews in American Wars* (Washington, D.C.: Jewish War Veterans of America, 1954), pp. 100–101.

45. Carl Sandburg, one of Americas best-loved poets, covered the turmoil for the *Chicago Daily News*. His articles were later collected in a book:

Carl Sandburg, *The Chicago Race Riots* (1919; reprint, New York: Harcourt Brace, 1969).

46. Quoted in Franklin, p. 20.

47. For different views on this period, see Nathaniel Weyl, *The Jew in American Politics* (New Rochelle, N.Y.: Arlington House, 1968), pp. 113–16; Liebman, pp. 55–59; and Howe, *World of Our Fathers*, pp. 325–30.

48. See Gorelick, p. 120.

49. For a concise description of the postwar period, see T. H. Watkins, *The Great Depression* (Boston: Little, Brown, 1993), pp. 23–47.

50. See Karp, p. 269.

51. Quoted in Karp, p. 271.

52. The National Association of Manufacturers and local chambers of commerce fought to keep the golden door open to low-cost immigrant labor and to fight unionization by creating an oversupply of workers.

53. Quoted in Karp, p. 266.

54. Quoted in Liebman, p. 423. Coolidge was subtle compared with others. In 1926, the House of Representatives Committee on Immigration endorsed the views of anti-Semitic American consuls, who were responsible for approving prospective immigrants' requests for authorization to enter America. "America faced an inundation of 'abnormally twisted' and unassimilable Jews—'filthy, un-American, and often dangerous in their habits,'" the consuls had said (quoted in Liebman, p. 425).

55. Liebman, p. 424.

56. For more on the wave of anti-Semitism in the 1920s, see Karp, pp. 266–74, and Gorelick, p. 140.

57. See Garza, *Women in Medicine*, p. 68.

58. Quoted in Gilbert G. Gonzalez, *Chicano Education in the Era of Segregation* (Philadelphia: Balch Institute Press, 1990), p. 88.

59. Karp, p. 274.

60. See Karp, pp. 282–84. For a lengthy treatment of Jews in the film industry, see Neil Gabler, *An Empire of Their Own: How the Jews Invented Hollywood* (New York: Crown, 1988).

61. Quoted in Cripps, p. 77.

62. Quoted in Karp, p. 251.

63. Quoted in Mari Jo Buhle, Paul Buhle, and Dan Georgakas, eds., *Encyclopedia of the American Left* (New York: Garland, 1990), p. 642.

64. Diner, p. 20.

65. Quoted in Diner, p. 43.

CHAPTER FOUR

1. For full details on this period, see T. H. Watkins, *The Great Depression* (Boston: Little, Brown, 1993).

2. Quoted in Watkins, p. 76.

3. For details on Harlem see Adam Clayton Powell, Jr., *Marching Blacks* (New York: Dial Press, 1945). A detailed work on the Communist Party in

Harlem on which most of the information for this chapter was based is Mark Naison, *Communists in Harlem during the Depression* (New York: Grove Press, 1984).

4. Quoted in Naison, p. 155.

5. For details, see Watkins, pp. 91-98.

6. Ford was the last auto plant in Detroit to unionize. In April 1941, when the United Auto Workers made a stand to unionize Ford's River Rouge plant, the head of Ford's police, Harry Bennett, recruited several hundred black workers from the South to break the strike and even physically assault the pickets. Many of these men later joined the union and realized that they had been used by Ford. For more details, see Robert Shogan and Tom Craig, *The Detroit Race Riot* (Philadelphia: Chilton Books, 1964).

7. No records were kept of the ethnic backgrounds of the recruiters, but participants later stated that Jewish youth were prominent among them. See Naison, pp. 321-22. Even so, according to Feuerlicht (p. 126), Jewish Communists never made up more than 1.5 percent of the 4.5 million Jews in America.

8. Naison, p. 31.

9. See also Mari Jo Buhle, Paul Buhle, and Dan Georgakas, eds., *Encyclopedia of the American Left* (New York: Garland, 1990), pp. 366-67.

10. Many Harlem residents were upset, however, when they heard people in the ILD and Unemployed Council make unfavorable remarks about non-Communist black leaders like A. Philip Randolph and W. E. B. Du Bois. Randolph had stated publicly that Soviet ruler Joseph Stalin had forgotten all about democracy. This enraged the Communists, who disrupted a conference on unemployment called by Randolph and his supporters.

11. Buhle, Buhle, and Georgakas, p. 684. The Scottsboro case has been covered in detail in many books, including Naison, pp. 57-89, and Watkins, pp. 89-91.

12. "The trial was a mockery and the boys are in danger of losing their lives only because they are Negroes," the *Forward* editorialized (quoted in Hasia R. Diner, *In the Almost Promised Land: American Jews and Blacks, 1915-1935* [Westport, Conn.: Greenwood Press, 1977], p. 412).

13. Quoted in Naison, p. 81.

14. The *Amsterdam News* warned the executive secretary of the NAACP, "Walter White, this is your last chance" (quoted in Naison, p. 83).

15. More complete information on early black response may be found in Gabrielle Simon Edgcomb, *From Swastika to Jim Crow: Refugee Scholars at Black Colleges* (Malabar, Fla.: Krieger, 1993), and Lunabelle Wedlock, *The Reaction of Negro Publications and Organizations to German Anti-Semitism* (Washington, D.C.: Howard University Press, 1942).

16. Quoted in Wedlock, p. 111.

17. The list is reproduced in Edgcomb, pp. 11-16.

18. An exception was the New School for Social Research in New York City, which established a University in Exile and hired several refugee scholars.

19. Quoted in Virginia Hamilton, *Paul Robeson: The Life and Times of a Free Black Man* (New York: Harper & Row, 1974).

20. Congressmen are permitted to debate bills without time limits. When they desire to kill the possibilities of a bill's passage, they can literally talk it to death, or filibuster, until the legislation is dropped. Only a two-thirds vote can end the filibuster and force a vote.

21. Quoted in Naison, p. 107.

22. In 1928, Jewish voters on the Lower East Side had overwhelmingly supported Catholic Al Smith in his bid for the presidency, giving him 72 percent of their votes. Smith had a liberal record in the state assembly, where he had introduced bills for better conditions for workers after the Triangle fire. For details, see Feuerlicht, pp. 119-20.

23. An area in the Bronx where black women gathered in the morning waiting to be hired for a day's cleaning work by middle-class white women, who were assumed to be from nearby Jewish neighborhoods. Wealthy women seldom came there for household help; they had full-time servants working in their homes.

24. See Wedlock, p. 23.

25. Quoted in Wedlock, p. 9.

26. Jonathan Kaufman, *Broken Alliance* (New York: New American Library, 1988), pp. 53-54.

27. Naison, p. 214.

28. In New York and Chicago, the ILGWU launched a major unionization campaign in 1933, hiring black organizers and recruiting thousands of African American garment workers to the union's predominantly Jewish ranks. In 1935, Jewish labor leaders joined with Frank Crosswaith, a close associate of A. Philip Randolph, and formed the Harlem Labor League, a federation of all black unionists. The new organization fought for and won the admission of African Americans to several unions. At a New York Negro Labor Conference that year, black leaders praised "officers and members of ILGWU upon its edifying example of labor solidarity" (quoted in Diner, p. 202). When the National Negro Congress was founded in 1935, considerable support came from several predominantly Jewish trade unions. See also Naison, p. 183.

29. In New Orleans, Italian shopkeepers in black neighborhoods were boycotted by similar campaigns. In Boston, Irish businessmen were the focus of black anger. See Robert G. Weisbord and Arthur Stein, *Bittersweet Encounter* (Westport, Conn.: Negro Universities Press, 1970), p. 79.

30. Weisbord and Stein, p. 46.

31. Quoted in Diner, p. 79.

32. Quoted in Diner, p. 80.

33. Originally, a national health plan was part of the proposals, but the American Medical Association applied enormous pressure to make sure it would not be included in future legislation. Watkins, pp. 242-73, contains the story of the New Deal programs.

34. See Jack Salzman, ed., *Bridges and Boundaries* (New York: Braziller, 1992), p. 206.

35. For details, see Naison, pp. 140-41.

36. Quoted in Naison, p. 215.

37. Racially derogatory readers and textbooks were replaced, and black history was taught in the classrooms. The tracking system was weakened, and more children were encouraged to take college preparatory courses. The tracking system meant that it was decided in the early grades which children were not college material. The commercial curriculum for these children did not contain subjects necessary for college admission.

38. Quoted in Neil Gabler, *An Empire of their Own: How the Jews Invented Hollywood* (New York: Crown, 1988), p. 2.

39. As one film critic explained it, "They were wary of offending the Gentiles and losing their audiences. As a result they avoided Jewish subjects, provided little work for Jewish character actors, and Anglicized the names of Jewish stars...." From Leonard Quart, "The Triumph of Assimilation: Ethnicity, Race and the Jewish Moguls," *Cineaste*, v. xviii, 1991, pp. 8-11.

40. Quotes are from Gabler, p. 319.

41. Quoted in Frank J. Donner, *The Un-Americans* (New York: Ballantine Books, 1961), p. 21.

42. Quoted in Feuerlicht, p. 125.

43. Feuerlicht, p. 125.

44. For the full story of America's farmworkers during the Great Depression, see Watkins, pp. 189-213, 291-94, and the PBS documentary based on Watkins' book, *The Great Depression*.

45. For details, see Watkins, pp. 277-88.

46. For more details, see Hedda Garza, *Francisco Franco* (New York: Chelsea House, 1987).

47. The full story of Joe Louis is told in the PBS documentary, *The Great Depression*. In 1908, another African American boxer, Jack Johnson, had won the world heavyweight championship and held it for seven years. then a concerted effort had been made to keep black boxers out of the limelight.

48. For further details see Naison, 193-95.

49. Quoted in Naison, p. 195.

50. Quoted in Naison, p. 197.

51. Quoted in Naison, p. 198.

52. Quoted in Naison, p. 264.

53. For further details, see Naison, pp. 264-65.

54. Naison, p. 261.

55. In the spring of 1939, the Coordinating Committee won a battle for jobs for blacks at the New York World's Fair and then vanished from the scene as World War II closed in. See Naison, p. 272.

56. Quoted in Naison, p. 272.

CHAPTER FIVE

1. Quoted in Gabrielle Simon Edgcomb, *From Swastika to Jim Crow: Refugee Scholars at Black Colleges* (Malabar, Fla.: Krieger, 1993), p. 19.

2. For more details, see Edgcomb, p. 19.

3. Quoted in Edgcomb, p. 19.

4. Information on U.S. policy during the Holocaust against the Jews is based on David S. Wyman, *The Abandonment of the Jews* (New York: Pantheon, 1985), and on the PBS documentary *America and the Holocaust*, available on videotape.

5. For a detailed analysis of this response, see Lunabelle Wedlock, *The Reaction of Negro Publications and Organizations to German Anti-Semitism* (Washington, D.C.: Howard University, 1942).

6. One article from a Nazi publication, *Das Schwarze Korps*, on November 24, 1938, warned the democracies that their professed compassion for German Jews was not reflected in their immigration policies. The NAACP journal *The Crisis* of February 1939 pointed out the difference between blacks in the United States and Jews in Germany. Blacks had "the right to protest and work to improve their lot. In Germany Jews have no such privilege. There is no hope" (quoted in Edgcomb, p. 48).

7. This chapter's information on the fight against segregation in the military is based on Richard M. Dalfiume, *Desegregation of the U.S. Armed Forces—Fighting on Two Fronts, 1939-1953* (Columbia: University of Missouri Press, 1969).

8. Quoted in Arthur Liebman, *Jews and the Left* (New York: Wiley, 1979), p. 508.

9. Quoted in Robert G. Weisbord and Arthur Stein, *Bittersweet Encounter* (Westport, Conn.: Negro Universities Press, 1970), p. 60.

10. Quoted in S. Carl Hirsch, *The Riddle of Racism* (New York: Viking Press, 1972), p. 42.

11. For details on World War II battles, see Tom McGowen, *World War II* (New York: Franklin Watts, 1993).

12. President Roosevelt ordered the War Department to prepare a statement that "colored men will have equal opportunity with white men in all departments of the army." The Army agreed that 10 percent of its men—36,000 of the first 400,000 draftees—would be African Americans, who would serve in segregated units, of course, and that the army would soon develop all-black air units (quoted in Dalfiume, p. 36).

13. Supreme Court Associate Justice Felix Frankfurter, was urged by Walter White to recommend Hastie for that post. Frankfurter had been Hastie's law professor at Harvard.

14. Quoted in Dalfiume, p. 42.

15. Quoted in Dalfiume, p. 57.

16. Quoted in Dalfiume, p. 57.

17. "Textbooks in Mississippi," *Opportunity*, April 1940, p. 99.

18. Walter White visited the men of the all-black Second Cavalry Division in North Africa and reported that the men were extremely discouraged. He contacted Eleanor Roosevelt and proposed the idea of a volunteer integrated combat division. Mrs. Roosevelt futilely presented the plan to the president and General George Marshall. Once again White wrote to Felix

Frankfurter, urging him to intervene, but the War Department would not budge from its firm refusal.

19. Quoted in Dalfiume, p. 55.

20. Quoted in Dalfiume, p. 47.

21. Quoted in Dalfiume, p. 60.

22. In Tucson, Arizona, for example, the government offered to pay $50,000 for the construction of a recreational center for black troops, but the townspeople voted the proposal down rather than have nonwhites near their city. Even in army hospitals and barbershops, the National American Legion commander protested the presence of black soldiers. The Army General Staff reported that black troops were unwanted at five out of six northern army camps.

23. Before Pearl Harbor, in a wooded area at Fort Benning, Georgia, Private Felix Hall was found hanging from a tree with his hands tied behind his back. Army authorities were ridiculed when they called Hall a suicide and never found the criminals.

24. Quoted in Dalfiume, p. 68.

25. Quoted in Wyman, p. 13.

26. For details on Jews in the military during World War II, see J. George Fredman and Louis A. Falk, *Jews in American Wars* (Washington, D.C.: Jewish War Veterans of the United States of America, 1954), pp. 103-227.

27. For more details, see Howard Zinn, *A People's History of the United States* (New York: Harper Perennial, 1980), pp. 398-426; and Donald R. McCoy and Richard T. Ruetten, *Quest and Response* (Wichita: University Press of Kansas, 1978), pp. 4-6.

28. Quoted in Fredman and Falk, p. 218.

29. See Wyman, pp. 11-14.

30. In his book *Marching Blacks* (New York: Dial Press, 1945), p. 114, Powell comments, "The Ku Klux Klan tried to sell itself to blacks on the grounds that it was against Jews only. Likewise, the Bund let it be known that they were not primarily against black folk. The America First Committee actively sought the support of black individuals and organizations. But the blacks remained steadfastedly loyal. What a great lesson this was for the American conscience! . . . America's fifth column included in its rank senators, representatives, generals, admirals, financiers, and national heroes—but not the name of one marching black."

31. Quoted in Weisbord, p. 62.

32. Quoted in Wyman, p. 46.

33. Quoted in Edgcomb, p. 125.

34. This statement is reproduced in Jack Salzman, ed., *Bridges and Boundaries* (New York: Braziller, 1992), p. 213.

35. The riots began with skirmishes between sailors and marines on shore leave in Los Angeles and teenage Mexican Americans and African Americans, so-called zoot-suiters because of the long jackets, wide-brimmed

hats, and narrow-cuff peg pants they wore. On June 7, the disturbances escalated into a full-scale race war, as uniformed white sailors entered movie houses and bars looking for anyone with a dark skin—Mexicans, blacks and Filipinos. The navy eventually issued orders prohibiting sailors from entering Mexican neighborhoods. For details see James D. Cockcroft, *The Hispanic Struggle for Social Justice* (New York: Franklin Watts, 1994).

36. See Powell, pp. 160-161.

37. For details and background on the rioting in Detroit, see Robert Shogan and Tom Craig, *The Detroit Race Riot* (Philadelphia: Chilton Books, 1964).

38. Quoted in Shogan and Craig, p. 31.

39. Writer John Roy Carlson masqueraded as a Nazi sympathizer while researching his exposé of America's fascists. He learned about the National Workers League's tactics from an ex-convict named Tony Bommarito: "You begins your work by talking against the Jews and the niggers. The Jew got us into the war. You tell 'em that.... It's the Jew who hires niggers and gives them low wages. You ties in the niggers with the Jew, den you call the Jews Communists" (quoted in Shogan and Craig, p. 28).

40. See A. Russell Buchanan, *Black Americans in World War II* (Santa Barbara, Calif.: Clio Books, 1977), pp. 45-57.

41. Quoted in Shogan and Craig, p. 40.

42. Quoted in Powell, pp. 162-63.

43. Shogan and Craig, p. 91.

44. Quoted in Powell, pp. 166-67.

45. See Shogan and Craig, p. 93.

46. The poorly financed War Refugee Board was headed by Secretary of War Stimson, by then a master of delaying tactics. Jewish leaders pleaded with the government to at least bomb the gas chambers at Auschwitz, but although American bombers had targeted a German war plant five miles from the concentration camp, the military claimed that Auschwitz was a strategically impossible target.

47. In February 1943, the Germans were stopped at Stalingrad, in the Soviet Union, when the people of that city fought back in the bitter cold. Russian armies pushed after the fleeing Nazis in a huge offensive. By summer, American and British forces landed on the island of Sicily off the southern coast of Italy. By fall, the Italian government had signed an armistice. In the Pacific, a campaign began to retake the Japanese-held Pacific Islands. For details, see McGowen.

48. Author's personal interview, 1987.

49. Zinn, p. 406.

50. For the full story of the black tank battalions, called the Panthers, see Lou Potter, *Liberators* (New York: Harcourt Brace Jovanovich, 1992), pp. 58-154.

51. Quoted in Wyman, p. 13.

52. Quoted in Potter, p. 221.

CHAPTER SIX

1. The principal sources on the post-World War II period were Donald R. McCoy and Richard T. Ruetten, *Quest and Response. Minority Rights and the Truman Administration* (Wichita: University Press of Kansas, 1973); Richard M. Dalfiume, *Desegregation of the Armed Forces: Fighting on Two Fronts, 1939-1953* (Columbia: University of Missouri Press, 1969); Howard Zinn, *A People's History of the United States* (New York: Harper Perennial, 1980), pp. 409-34.

2. *New York Times*, December 1, 1946, quoted in Dalfiume.

3. Walter White wrote that "Negro militancy and implacable determination to wipe out segregation grew more proportionately during the years 1940-45 than during any other period of the Negro's history in America" (quoted in McCoy and Reutten, p. 11).

4. See Jonathan Kaufman, *Broken Alliance* (New York: New American Library), p. 44.

5. Quoted in McCoy and Ruetten, p. viii. For details, see McCoy and Reutten, pp. 1-8.

6. When Mexican Americans in California sued against school segregation, supporting testimony (amici curiae) was filed by several organizations including the NAACP and the American Jewish Congress. In San Antonio, Texas, black and Mexican voters joined together and elected an African American to the board of trustees of a junior college and a Mexican American to a local school board. As Japanese Americans struggled to erase the effects of the terrible wartime propaganda campaign against them, the *Afro-American* editorialized that "American prejudice and hatred of Japanese Americans is one of the blackest pages in our history" (quoted in McCoy and Reutten, p. 65). For more on the Latinos' very active role in the 1940s and early 1950s, see James D. Cockcroft, *The Hispanic Struggle for Social Justice* (New York: Franklin Watts, 1994), Chapter 5.

7. Quoted in McCoy and Ruetten, p. 29.

8. For more, see Hedda Garza, "Bring the Boys Home," in *American History Illustrated*, June 1985, pp. 36-41; and Zinn, pp. 417-19.

9. Quoted in McCoy and Ruetten, p. 48.

10. Quoted in Dalfiume, p. 52.

11. Quoted in Zinn, p. 440.

12. Quoted in McCoy and Ruetten, p. 37.

13. Quoted in McCoy and Reutten, p. 71.

14. Legislatures in Connecticut, New Jersey, and New York established fair employment practices commissions. Without fanfare, the American Red Cross blood banks distributed blood plasma without racial labeling, although records were kept for the benefit of physicians requesting such information. Articles on the problems of America's racial minorities slowly started appearing in popular news and women's magazines. Here and there in the slim ranks of black professionals, gains were made. In 1946, black nurses were permitted to join the American Nurses Association in several states where

they had been excluded from membership. By 1947, a handful of African American journalists held jobs with white-owned newspapers, and a handful of black professors were hired by white colleges along with previously excluded Jewish and Catholic teachers.

15. Quoted in Kaufman, pp. 82–83.

16. For more details, see Hank Greenberg, *The Story of My Life*, ed., Ira Berkow (New York: Times Books, 1989).

17. Quoted in Greenberg, p. 191.

18. Quoted in McCoy and Reutten, p. 166. No one expected Walt Disney to change his policies. It had long been reported that Disney refused to hire Jews. For more details, see Neil Gabler, *An Empire of Their Own: How the Jews Invented Hollywood* (New York: Crown, 1988), p. 364.

19. Among the movies were *Lost Boundaries* and *Pinky*, about blacks passing for white, although the latter film starred a white actress; *Intruder in the Dust*, about the horrors of lynching; and *Home of the Brave*, about racism against black soldiers during World War II.

20. Quoted in McCoy and Reutten, p. 167.

21. The information on HUAC's investigation of Hollywood is based on material in Patricia Erens, *The Jew in American Cinema*, Bloomington: Indiana University Press, 1984; and Gabler.

22. Quoted in Gabler, p. 356.

23. Quoted in Gabler, p. 357.

24. Quotes in this section are from Gabler, p. 170.

25. Gabler, p. 367.

26. Quoted in Victor S. Navasky, *Naming Names* (New York: Viking Press, 1980), p. 369.

27. Quoted in Gabler, p. 379.

28. Lillian Hellman, a playwright who later refused to testify before HUAC, commented that the Jewish producers were foreign-born and had done what would "not have been possible in Russia or Poland. It was possible here to offer the cossacks a bowl of chicken soup to save themselves from the wrath of the anti-Semites, [and] that is what they did" (quoted in Gabler, p. 374).

29. This section is based on Richard Kluger, *Simple Justice: The History of* Brown *v.* Board of Education *and Black America's Struggle for Equality* (New York: Knopf, 1976), pp. 388–90. The quotes are taken from the same source.

30. Before Wallace even declared his candidacy, the *Negro Digest* in May 1946 published a poll claiming that 91 percent of black voters wanted Wallace as the Democratic Party nominee for president in 1948. Also, at the Democratic National Convention of 1944, black delegates had supported Wallace's nomination for vice president against Truman's.

31. Quoted in McCoy and Reutten, p. 133.

32. The *Nation*, Aug. 20, 1948.

33. Quoted in McCoy and Reutten, p. 134.

34. The *Chicago Defender* told its black readers, "In order to love him [Wallace], you must also love his motley crew of Communist stooges, for he has refused to repudiate the Commies" (quoted in McCoy and Reutten, p. 135).

35. Quoted in McCoy and Reutten, p. 187.

36. When a few schoolchildren dared to say in class that furniture was no protection against atomic radiation or that the Soviet Union had many fine scientists, perfectly capable of inventing their own atomic bomb, they found themselves in the principal's office, waiting for their parents to come to school to answer for their "disloyal" remarks. Author's personal experience in the early 1950s.

37. For more details, see Rebecca Larsen, *Hero Before His Time* (New York: Franklin Watts, 1989), pp. 119-24; and Howard Fast, *Peekskill: USA* (New York: Civil Rights Congress, 1951).

38. Quoted in Fast, p. 120.

39. Quoted in Fast, p. 34.

40. Quoted in Fast, p. 103.

41. Quoted in Fast, p. 127.

42. A major source on McCarthy is Frank J. Donner, *The Un-Americans* (New York: Ballantine Books, 1961).

43. For more on the Korean War, see Zinn, pp. 419-21.

44. In November 1948, Thomas had been indicted for conspiracy to defraud the government. He had paid the salaries to two nonexistent aides. He was eventually sentenced to a jail term and sent to a federal prison where, ironically, one of his prison mates was Ring Lardner, Jr., one of the Hollywood Ten.

45. Quoted in Donner, p. 34.

46. For details, see Navasky, pp. 186-94.

47. From *One Lonely Night*, a best-selling 1951 novel by Spillane.

48. Quoted in McCoy and Reutten, p. 293.

49. For details on Du Bois's later years, see Patricia and Frederick McKissack, *W. E. B. Du Bois* (New York: Franklin Watts, 1990), pp. 103-19.

50. Quoted in Donner, p. 35.

51. The founder of the John Birch Society, Robert Welch, considered ex-President Eisenhower and 7,000 of the nation's Protestant ministers "Reds." Clardy once said he wanted to "have...the right to put witnesses down in the dungeon underneath the Capitol if they refused to cooperate with the committee" (quoted in Donner, p. 40).

52. Quoted in Donner, p. 41.

53. Scherer called Congressman Roosevelt's remark "a paraphrase of a remark I have heard time and time again since serving on the Committee. It has come repeatedly from sullen, defiant, and contemptuous members of the Communist party.... [It] makes me wonder if he actually wrote the particular remarks" (quoted in Donner, p. 38).

54. Quoted in Dorothy Sterling, *Tear Down the Walls!* (Garden City, N.Y.: Doubleday, 1968), p. 169.

CHAPTER SEVEN

1. The information in this chapter is based on several books: Dorothy Sterling, *Tear Down the Walls!* (Garden City: Doubleday, 1968); Emma Gelders Sterne, *I Have a Dream* (New York: Knopf, 1965); Henry Hampton, Steve Fayer, and Sarah Flynn, *Voices of Freedom: An Oral History of the Civil Rights Movement from the 1950s through the 1980s* (New York: Bantam Books, 1990); Langston Hughes and Milton Meltzer, *African American History* (New York: Scholastic, 1990); James Peck, *Freedom Ride* (New York: Simon & Schuster, 1962); David J. Garrow, *Bearing the Cross* (New York: Vintage Books, 1988); and Howard Zinn, *A People's History of the United States* (New York: Harper Perennial, 1980), pp. 441-59. Other books on specific aspects of that era are cited in later notes.

2. The NAACP raised funds and opened an account in a black-owned bank to meet some of the financial needs of these parents.

3. For details, see especially Garrow, pp. 11-82.

4. The Reverend George Lee, the first black to register to vote in his county, had died when a shotgun was fired into his face just three months earlier. The week before Emmett arrived for his visit, another voter, Lamar Smith, was shot in broad daylight in front of a courthouse in Brookhaven, Mississippi. (For details on the Till case and the testimony of many of the people involved, see Hampton, Fayer, and Flynn, pp. 1-15.)

5. The cousins did not tell their grandfather, Mose Wright, about the incident. Later, Curtis Jones said, "If we had...I'm sure he would have gotten us out of there" (quoted in Hampton, Fayer, and Flynn) p. 4.

6. Quoted in Hampton, Fayer, and Flynn, p. 6.

7. In Tuscaloosa, Alabama, by dint of a federal district court order, on Friday, February 3, 1956, Autherine Lucy attended her first class at the university. By Monday the white supremacists had organized to drive her away. Over a thousand rock throwers aimed their missiles at the automobile of the dean of women as she drove Autherine Lucy to class. The home of the college president was stoned, and the trustees voted to expel Lucy.

8. One of them, Ernest Green, needed the chemistry classes offered at Central High to qualify for college admission as a chemical engineering student. Terence Roberts, a straight-A student, optimistically said, "They'll like me when they get to know me."

Melba Pattillo Beals said that she "understood education before I understood anything else." Her mother had always told her, "Education is your key to survival." Central High had more equipment and "five floors of opportunities" (quote from Hampton, Fayer, and Flynn, pp. 38-39).

9. Quoted in Sterling, p. 174.

10. Quoted in Hampton, Fayer, and Flynn, p. 52.

11. In December, a Gallup poll listed the ten most admired men in the world. Along with Dr. Jonas Salk, discoverer of the polio vaccine, and world leaders like Sir Winston Churchill and President Dwight D. Eisenhower, appeared the name of Orval Faubus.

12. For details, see Conrad Lynn, *There Is a Fountain* (Brooklyn, N.Y.: Lawrence Hill Books, 1993), pp. 141–57.

13. In 1956, Williams and Perry had asked the city council to set aside one day a week in the town pool, built with WPA funds, for Monroe's black children. The town council refused, saying that they could not afford to drain the pool every week after the black swimmers polluted it. The Klan announced that they would burn down Dr. Perry's home, but as the Klansmen came down the road leading to it, Williams and other black men opened fire from treetops and trenches. The Klan left them alone after that, but the NAACP leadership was not too happy (see Lynn, pp. 142–43 for details), although the preamble to a resolution of the fiftieth convention of the NAACP, held in New York City in July 1959, reaffirmed "the right of an individual and collective self-defense against unlawful assaults" (quoted in Arnold Adoff, ed., *Black on Black: Commentaries by Negro Americans* [New York: Macmillan, 1968], p. 194).

14. Quoted in Lynn, pp. 154–55.

15. Quoted in Lynn, p. 157.

16. See Zinn, p. 445.

17. Peck, p. 7.

18. This is the theme of Donald R. McCoy and Richard T. Reutten's *Quest and Response: Minority Rights and the Truman Administration* (Wichita: University Press of Kansas, 1973).

19. Quoted in Peck, pp. 154–55.

20. Information on the fight-back against HUAC is based on Frank J. Donner, *The Un-Americans* (New York: Ballantine Books, 1961).

21. Cardinal Cushing said, "It [the McCarran-Walter Act] cannot be defended without recourse to the discredited and un-Christian tenet of racism" (quoted in Donner, p. 44).

22. Quoted in Donner, p. 44.

23. Dr. John A. McKay, president of Princeton Theological Seminary and moderator of the Presbyterian Church in the United States, called HUAC "the Twentieth Century American version of the Sixteenth Century Spanish Inquisition" (quoted in Donner, p. 244).

24. Quotes are from Donner, p. 177. Sherwood's widow said, "You (HUAC) have helped to kill my husband and make my four children fatherless. Throughout his lifetime my husband had but one goal—to ease the suffering of mankind. It was this goal that drew him to support the Loyalists in the Spanish Civil War, that inspired his youthful identification with radical causes. It was this goal that led him...to abandon politics completely and devote himself single mindedly to science. Is it a crime for a young man in his twenties to dream of a bright new world?" (quoted in Donner, p. 179).

25. Quoted in Donner, p. 193.

26. But Walters wasn't through yet. He instructed his staff to give his files on the teachers to local school boards. Six teachers were fired and several new teachers never received contracts. For details, see Donner, pp. 200–201.

27. Quoted in Donner, p. 203.

28. In Nashville, Tennessee, a dynamite blast destroyed a school where a black kindergarten child had registered. In Jacksonville, a bomb blew up the home of a black family whose six-year-old had enrolled in a white school. In New Orleans, when four black first-graders entered the school, a yearlong boycott took place. All public schools were closed, and a private segregated school financed by state taxes opened its doors in Prince Edward County, Virginia, leaving 1,700 black students with no schools to attend. Similar steps were taken throughout the South. By 1964, only 2.25 percent of the African American children of the South attended desegregated schools. A doctor who examined African American students who had chosen the white high school in Camden, Alabama, found them "shell-shocked" because of "extreme physical harassment" by their schoolmates (quoted in Sterling, p. 181).

29. Quoted in Sterling, p. 178.

30. Quoted in Sterling, p. 49.

31. Jack Nelson, then Atlanta bureau chief of the *Los Angeles Times*, was covering the South full time. He had this to say about his home state of Mississippi: "It had become a dark and fearful place, violently obsessed with race, a virtual police state. Civil rights advocates were hounded throughout the South, but only in Mississippi did the state government maintain a network of surveillance, coercion and control to preserve the status quo. Working together, the tax-supported Mississippi Sovereignty Commission and the private White Citizens Councils were able to crush even the most modest forms of dissent." See Jack Nelson, *Terror in the Night: The Klan's Campaign Against the Jews* (New York: Simon & Schuster, 1993), p. 11.

32. Jonathan Kaufman, *Broken Alliance* (New York: New American Library, 1988), p. 94.

33. The story and its quoted passages is from William Bradford Huie, *Three Lives for Mississippi* (New York: WCC Books, 1964), pp. 13–14.

34. Quoted in Irving Howe, *World of Our Fathers* (New York: Harcourt Brace Jovanovich, 1976), p. 631.

35. Arthur Liebman, *Jews and the Left* (New York: Wiley, 1979), pp. 545–55.

36. Quoted in Kaufman, p. 105.

37. Kaufman, p. 105.

38. Quoted in Nelson, p. 63.

39. Huie, p. 36. The story of Chaney, Goodman, and Schwerner is based on Seth Cagin and Philip Dray, *We Are Not Afraid* (New York: Macmillan, 1988).

40. See Nelson, p. 12.

41. See Huie, p. 107.

42. Huie, p. 227.

43. Quotes are from Huie, pp. 231-32.

44. Quoted in Huie, p. 231.

45. Huie, p. 245.

46. For the full story of the free speech movement, see W. J. Rorabaugh, *Berkeley at War: The 1960s* (New York: Oxford University Press, 1989), and Hedda Garza, *Joan Baez* (New York: Chelsea House, 1991), pp. 16, 18, 26.

47. See Liebman, p. 67.

48. See Garrow, p. 413.

49. Quoted in Garrow, p. 439.

50. See Sterling, p. 181.

51. Quoted in Adoff, pp. 210-12.

52. From the *New York Post*, June 23, 1967, quoted in Liebman, p. 231.

53. Howe, p. 632.

54. Although the number of Jewish students on college campuses averaged about 325,000 each year, most of them were not involved in SDS. At the SDS convention in 1966, some 46 percent identified themselves as Jewish. Liebman also reports: "In a major study of student activism conducted by the American Council of Education during the 1966-1967 school year, a Jewish background was the single most important predictor of participation in antiwar or antiadministration protests. An estimated one-third to one-half of most committed activists at the most volatile schools were Jews." See Liebman, pp. 67-68.

55. For details, see Robert Weisbord, *Bittersweet Encounter*. (Westport: Negro University Press, 1970), pp. 139-160.

56. Quoted in Weisbord, p. 141.

57. Quoted in Kaufman, p. 166.

58. Quoted in Garrow, p. 527.

59. Quoted in Zinn, pp. 451-52.

60. The author worked as an interviewer in Harlem for the film crew that produced *No Vietnamese Ever Called Me Nigger*, David Weiss's prize-winning documentary of the 1967 demonstration. During the march, a contingent of high school girls paraded by. A white prowar cameraman commented bitterly: "Look at the Jewish virgins!"

61. Quoted in Max Geltman, *The Confrontation: Black Power, Anti-Semitism and the Myth of Integration* (Englewood Cliffs, N.J.: Prentice-Hall, 1970), p. 26.

62. See Kaufman, p. 77.

63. Quoted in Kaufman, p. 78.

64. See Kaufman, p. 78.

65. For details, see Nelson, pp. 45-48.

66. Quoted in Nelson, p. 68.

67. Quoted in Zinn, p. 453.

68. Quoted in Geltman, p. 194.

69. For details, see Zinn, p. 455.

CHAPTER EIGHT

1. Quoted in Jack Nelson, *Terror in the Night* (New York: Simon and Schuster, 1993), p. 270.

2. For details, see Victor S. Navasky, *Naming Names* (New York: The Viking Press, 1980), pp. 326-29.

3. Navasky, p. 239.

4. See Irving Howe, *World of Our Fathers* (New York: Harcourt Brace Jovanovich, 1976), pp. 634-36.

5. Quoted in Clarence Lusane, *The Struggle for Equal Education* (New York: Franklin Watts, 1992), p. 94. For more on the backlash, see James D. Cockcroft, *Latinos in the Struggle for Equal Education* (New York: Franklin Watts, 1995), Chapter 6; and Susan Faludi, *Backlash* (New York: Crown Publishers, Inc., 1991).

6. For details, see *New York Times*, June 3, 1994.

7. Howe, p. 611.

8. See Ann G. Wolfe, "The Invisible Jewish Poor," in Naomi Levine and Martin Hochbaum, eds., *Poor Jews: An American Awakening* (New Brunswick: Transaction Books, 1974), pp. 26-37; and Phyllis Franck, "The Hasidic Poor in New York City," pp. 59-69 in the same volume.

9. One authority calls U.S. housing policies a way of "sorting out winners and losers." See Gregory D. Squires, *Capital and Communities in Black and White* (Albany: State University of New York Press, 1994), p. 107.

10. Bernard Sanders, "Whither American Democracy," *Los Angeles Times*, January 16, 1994.

11. *New York Times*, May 23, 1994.

12. *New York Times*, October 26, 1994, p. A19.

13. *New York Times*, July 29, 1992, p. A15.

14. "Why NAACP Won't Disown Nation of Islam," letter signed by Gerald Horne, and Belle Zeller visiting professor of public policy, Brooklyn College, CUNY, in *New York Times*, Jan. 19, 1994. In fact, Malcolm X began speaking at socialist forums composed largely of whites. See George Breitman, *The Last Year of Malcolm X* (New York: Pathfinder, 1967).

15. Quoted in Pierre Clavel and Wim Wiewel, eds., *Harold Washington and the Neighborhoods: Progressive City Government in Chicago, 1983-1987* (New Brunswick, N.J.: Rutgers University Press, 1991), p. 145. For more information, see Cockcroft, Chapter 6.

16. Quoted from Bridge Builders brochure, kindly furnished by attorney Martin H. Belsky of Albany, New York.

17. With permission of the author, Eli Smith.

BIBLIOGRAPHY

Books especially recommended for students are marked with an asterisk (*).

Baum, Charlotte, Paula Hyman, and Sonya Michel. *The Jewish Woman in America*. New York: Dial Press, 1976.

*Cockcroft, James D. *The Hispanic Struggle for Social Justice*. New York: Franklin Watts, 1994.

Cripps, Thomas. *Slow Fade to Black: The Negro in American Film, 1900-1942*. New York: Oxford University Press, 1977.

Dalfiume, Richard M. *Desegregation of the U.S. Armed Forces—Fighting on Two Fronts, 1939-1953*. Columbia: University of Missouri Press, 1969.

Diner, Hasia R. *In the Almost Promised Land: American Jews and Blacks, 1915-1935*. Westport, Conn.: Greenwood Press, 1977.

*Donner, Frank J. *The Un-Americans*. New York: Ballantine Books, 1961.

Edgcomb, Gabrielle Simon. *From Swastika to Jim Crow: Refugee Scholars at Black Colleges*. Malabar, Fla.: Krieger, 1993.

*Fast, Howard. *Peekskill: USA*. New York: Civil Rights Congress, 1951.

*Gabler, Neil. *An Empire of Their Own: How the Jews Invented Hollywood*. New York: Crown, 1988.

*Garrow, David J. *Bearing the Cross*. New York: Vintage Books, 1988.

*Garza, Hedda. *Latinas: Hispanic Women in the United States*. New York: Franklin Watts, 1994.

*———. *Women in Medicine*. New York: Franklin Watts, 1994.

Gorelick, Sherry. *City College and the Jewish Poor*. New Brunswick, N.J.: Rutgers University Press, 1981.

*Greenberg, Hank. *The Story of My Life*, ed. Ira Berkow. New York: Times Books, 1989.

*Hamilton, Virginia. *Paul Robeson: The Life and Times of a Free Black Man*. New York: Harper & Row, 1974.

*Hampton, Henry, Steve Fayer, and Sarah Flynn. *Voices of Freedom: An Oral History of the Civil Rights Movement from the 1950s Through the 1980s*. New York: Bantam Books, 1990.

*Hansen, Joyce. *Between Two Fires*. New York: Franklin Watts, 1993.

Higham, John. *Send These to Me: Immigrants in Urban America*. Baltimore: Johns Hopkins University Press, 1984.

*Howe, Irving. *World of Our Fathers*. New York: Harcourt Brace Jovanovich, 1976.

*Hughes, Langston, and Milton Meltzer. *African American History*. New York: Scholastic, 1990.

Jacobs, Paul, and Saul Landau, with Eve Pell. *To Serve the Devil*. New York: Vintage Books, 1971.

*Karp, Abraham J. *Haven and Home: A History of Jews in America*. New York: Schocken Books, 1985.

*Kaufman, Jonathan. *Broken Alliance*. New York: New American Library, 1988.

*Kluger, Richard. *Simple Justice: The History of* Brown *v.* Board of Education *and Black America's Struggle for Equality*. New York: Knopf, 1976.

*Larsen, Rebecca. *Hero before His Time*. New York: Franklin Watts, 1989.

*Libo, Kenneth, and Irving Howe. *We Lived There Too*. New York: St. Martin's-Marek, 1984.

Liebman, Arthur. *Jews and the Left*. New York: Wiley, 1979.

*Lynn, Conrad. *There Is a Fountain*. Brooklyn, N.Y.: Lawrence Hill Books, 1993.

McCoy, Donald R., and Richard T. Ruetten. *Quest and Response*. Wichita: University Press of Kansas, 1978.

*McGowen, Tom. *World War II*. New York: Franklin Watts, 1993.

*McKissack, Patricia, and Frederick McKissack. *W. E. B. Du Bois*. New York: Franklin Watts, 1990.

*Manners, Ande. *Poor Cousins*. New York: Coward, McCann & Geoghegan, 1972.

Meyers, Gerald. *Vito Marcantonio*. Albany: State University of New York Press, 1989.

Naison, Mark. *Communists in Harlem During the Depression*. New York: Grove Press, 1984.

Navasky, Victor S. *Naming Names*. New York: Viking Press, 1980.

Novotny, Anne. *Strangers at the Door*. New York: Bantam Books, 1974.

Peck, James. *Freedom Ride*. New York: Simon Schuster, 1962.

*Potter, Lou. *Liberators*. New York: Harcourt Brace Jovanovich, 1992.

Powell, Adam Clayton, Jr. *Marching Blacks*. New York: Dial Press, 1945.

*Salzman, Jack, ed. *Bridges and Boundaries: African Americans and American Jews*. New York: Braziller, 1992.

Shogan, Robert, and Tom Craig. *The Detroit Race Riot*. Philadelphia: Chilton Books, 1964.

*Sterling, Dorothy. *Tear Down the Walls! A History of the American Civil Rights Movement*. Garden City, N.Y.: Doubleday, 1968.

*Sterne, Emma Gelders. *I Have a Dream*. New York: Knopf, 1965.

*Watkins, T. H. *The Great Depression*. Boston: Little, Brown, 1993.

Wedlock, Lunabelle. *The Reaction of Negro Publications and Organizations to German Anti-Semitism*. Washington, D.C.: Howard University, 1942.

Weisbord, Robert G., and Arthur Stein. *Bittersweet Encounter*. Westport, Conn.: Negro Universities Press, 1970.

West, Cornel, and Michael Lerner. *Jews and Blacks: Let the Healing Begin*. New York: Putnam, 1995.

Wyman, David S. *The Abandonment of the Jews*. New York: Pantheon, 1985.

*Zinn, Howard. *A People's History of the United States*. New York: Harper Perennial, 1980.

VIDEOS*

Some of the postwar antiracist films mentioned in Chapter 5 are also available on videotape including, *Home of the Brave*, *Lost Boundaries*, and *Gentleman's Agreement*. Only a few of the many videos available on the subjects covered in this book are listed. In general, lesser known ones were selected.

On Early Jewish Immigrants: *Hester Street* (1975); *Ragtime* (1981)

On Slavery and the Civil War: *Mandingo* (1965); *Freedom Road* (1979); *The Civil War* (PBS, 1993); *The Autobiography of Miss Jane Pittman*, (1974)

On the Depression: *The Great Depression* (PBS, 1993)

On the Witch-hunt and the Cold War: *Point of Order* (1964); *The Front* (1976); *Fellow Traveler* (1990); *Daniel* (1983)

On the Holocaust: *America in the Holocaust* (PBS, 1994); *Schindler's List* (1994)

On Civil Rights: *Eyes on the Prize* (PBS, 1993); *Murder in Mississippi* (1990); *The Long Walk Home* (1990)

INDEX

African-American press: and anti-lynching movement, 115-116; and anti-Semitism, 79, 94; and military segregation, 110; on Nazism, 72-73; on radical groups, 90; and Scottsboro case, 70; and Till murder, 137

African Americans: alliances with Jewish Americans, *see* Black-Jewish alliance, Civil Rights movement; during American Revolution, 25-26; and anti-Semitism, *see* Black anti-Semitism; and anti-slavery movement, 29-30; and Civil War, 25-28, 30-32, 36; and Communist Party, *see* Communist Party; and convict labor, 49; economic status, 64, 133, 170-171; and film industry, *see* Film industry; and Great Migration, 51-52; and HUAC, 131; and integration of baseball, 117-119; middle class, 52, 62, 70, 169, 170; and military, *see* Military segregation; and New Deal, 80-81, 89, 92; in North, 28, 31-32, 36, 51-52; in South, 38, 48-50, 89, 92; and Reconstruction, 37; and rise of Nazi Germany, 72-73; and Vietnam War, 159, 163, 165; white back-lash against, 167, 169. *See also* Employment discrimination; Free African Americans; Housing discrimination; Slavery; *and entries under* "Black"

American Revolution, 22-23, 24-25

Americanization, 42-43, 44, 47-48, 52, 58, 62-63

Anti-Semitism: and Americanization campaign, 47-48; in baseball, 118-119; causes of, 11-13, 17-18; during Civil War, 36; and colleges, 56; in colonial America, 20; and community control issue, 166-167; and employment discrimination, 44, 58; and film industry, 58-59, 82, 119; and Ford, 66; during Great Depression, 76, 78-79; and HUAC, 120, 121; King on, 13; and lynching of Frank, 48; and McCarthyism, 144; in military, 110-112; NAACP on, 105; post-World War II, 131; in 1920s, 55-58; pre-Civil War, 33-35; in Russia, 40-41; and socialist ideology, 55; in South, 157, 164; during World War I, 53-54; during World War II, 102-103. *See also* Black anti-Semitism; Holocaust; Immigration laws; Nazi Germany

South: African Americans living in, 37-38, 48-50, 101-102; during Great Depression, 65; Jewish Americans living in, 34-35, 105, 157
Southern Christian Leadership Conference, 138, 141, 158
Southern Tenant Farmworkers Union (STFU), 84-85
Soviet Union: and American Communist Party, 67, 70, 84; and Cold War, 115, 116, 126; collapse of, 169; German invasion of, 99-100; Moscow trials in, 90; and rise of Nazi Germany, 70; and Stalin-Hitler pact, 95
Spanish Civil War, 83, 86-87, 89
Stimson, Henry, 97, 98, 100-101, 110
Student Nonviolent Coordinating Committee (SNCC), 141-142, 143, 149, 158-161, 163, 164
Students for a Democratic Society, 161
Supreme Court decisions: on civil rights, 38, 138, 142, 169; Dred Scott case, 32; on New Deal programs, 85-86, 91. See also Brown v. Board of Education

Teachers: HUAC and, 144-145; Jewish, 55, 58, 74, 78
Terrorists, 131, 136, 145, 148, 149, 157, 159, 164, 165
Till, Emmett, 137-138, 140
Trade Union Unity League (TUUL), 66-67
Transport Workers Union (TWU), 74, 91
Truman, Harry S., 112; and civil rights, 114, 115-116, 123-125; and Cold War, 120-121, 144

Unemployed Councils, 66-67, 68, 76

Union movement: and African Americans, 49, 64, 67, 78, 89, 91-92; and anti-Semitism, 58; and black-Jewish alliance, 74; and Civil Rights movement, 158; and Cold War, 115, 133; in early U.S., 27; in Hollywood, 83; and Jewish immigrants, 46-47; post-World War I, 55; and Roosevelt, 85-86; and teachers, 44, 78, 166
United Front policy, 72, 80-82
United Nations, 117, 129
U.S. economy: after American Revolution, 27; after Civil War, 37, 38; and civil rights, 169; and Cold War, 115, 133; in 1920s, 57; and racism, 9-12, 48, 159, 170. See also Great Depression
Urban League, 51, 52, 64, 70, 110

Vietnam War, 159, 163, 165. See also Anti-Vietnam War movement
Voting Rights Act of 1965, 158-159

Wallace, George, 156, 158
War of 1812, 28-29, 34
Washington, Booker T., 49-50, 51
Washington, George, 25, 26
Washington, Harold D., 173
White backlash, 167, 169
White Citizens Councils, 135, 142
White, Walter, 97, 116, 120, 131
Williams, Robert, 140, 141, 159
Wise, Stephen, 104, 105, 109, 122
Woodard, Isaac, Jr., 113, 116
World War I, 51-54, 62
World War II, 99, 110-111, 112; causes of, 86-87, 93; racism and anti-Semitism during, 102-103; U.S. entry into, 100; See also Military segregation; Nazi Germany

Zionism, 59, 60